The Civilized Minute

KATE T. LEWIS

INFINITY
PUBLISHING

Copyright © 2010 by Kate T. Lewis

ISBN 0-7414-6209-5

Printed in the United States of America

Published October 2010

INFINITY PUBLISHING
1094 New DeHaven Street, Suite 100
West Conshohocken, PA 19428-2713
Toll-free (877) BUY BOOK
Local Phone (610) 941-9999
Fax (610) 941-9959
Info@buybooksontheweb.com
www.buybooksontheweb.com

INTRODUCTION

"There is no accomplishment so easy to acquire as politeness, and none more profitable."

George Bernard Shaw

The Civilized Minute is designed to guide professionals toward appropriate behavior. The language is direct and to the point. Your career is nothing to fool around with, so getting right to the meat of the matter is essential. I do not mince words about the things that can damage your reputation and your career. After reading this book, you will find yourself more efficient and productive. You won't waste time worrying over how to handle an interview, whether you did something right or wrong at the office Christmas party or work through the regret of an opportunity lost because you simply didn't know what to do. Think of this as your roadmap. Your gameplan. When *this* happens, I will do *that*. *The Civilized Minute* takes common workplace and career scenarios and uses the skills of business etiquette to ensure the outcome is in your favor. Business etiquette should make you look good and other people feel good all the while advancing the brand you represent. After reading this book, you will see a difference in the way you are treated by the people around you. Suddenly, you will become the go-to person when a client is unhappy or unsure and this makes you very valuable in your organization.

THE SILENT KILLER

Not knowing how to handle yourself with poise and confidence in the workplace is considered the silent killer of your career. It's silent because no one wants to tell you to wash your hair more often. And, people are reluctant to say outright that your terrible attitude is bringing down the entire team. So rather than make themselves feel uncomfortable, coworkers and friends simply move away. Managers and business owners have a lot to consider in order to make the company successful. They don't have time to worry about you drinking too much when you take a client out to dinner or if you are pleasant and conversational with a new customer while lunch is brought in. In the mind of management and the customer, it's all about service quality so impressing customers with thoughtful and proactive behavior is paramount.

Having poor social/people skills is a killer because business is about people. Sure, products and services are what *lead* you to a company, but it's the people that keep you there. Without knowing the ground rules for acceptable behavior, you are shooting in the dark when you try to connect with people – co-workers, your boss, clients, the cook at the coffee shop, the man that owns your favorite clothing store, etc. It's as simple as this: no one wants to be around people who are awkward and ill-mannered. When you lack the confidence that comes from feeling prepared, people notice. Unfortunately, that insecurity often comes across as rudeness. Imagine a sulky-faced teenager. They probably are not as unhappy as they act, they are probably just uncomfortable in their own skin. Hopefully, they will learn that in the business world people will shun those who are closed – arms crossed, face un-smiling, eyes cast downward, and defensive body stance.

Likely, you are not a celebrity or professional athlete and are not grounded in a career where embarrassing and unethical episodes run rampant. So, don't be confused by what main stream media deems typical or acceptable. Probably, you are surrounded by real people who go to work every day and perform their tasks to earn their living.

You can be sure these people are talking behind your back if you try out a little office romance or park right at the front door every day.

If showing no couth and grace at work is the silent killer, then doing your job with compassion, patience and discretion is your highway to heaven. Honest and ethical behavior is the first thing assumed in business when you present yourself with class and taste. Wouldn't it be a shocker to find out the nice guy from R&D who always remembers birthdays and wears starched khakis every day is the mastermind behind some credit application scam? If you win over a customer with the genuinely gracious and thoughtful touches to the service you provide, you will have to screw up big time for them to leave quickly. You will have given them the impression that you honestly want to do right by them, to be the best service provider in the industry and are willing to work through any obstacles. That's a big assumption on your customer's part, but that's just the way it works.

As you go through these 16 weeks, you won't find topics covered in your company handbook or listed in your job description. Mastering the new project management software is no big deal. You take a class, you read the Help pages and you've got it figured out. It's the other unknowns that crop up in your work life that create the most anxiety. What do you do if you've been asked to travel with the most obnoxious person on your team to a very traditional client's office? What do you do if your cube-mate raises his voice about 60 decibels when he talks on the phone? What do you do when you hold your hand out to shake the hand of a new coworker and find he doesn't have one?

This book covers the buzz killers and the building blocks of your career. These are the things you don't learn in school and are unlikely to hear from anyone but a business coach. These are the things people in business complain about but don't teach their up-and-coming associates. Consider yourself savvy for reading this book. If you put these tips in play and change your mindset from *me* to *my business*, you will have launched the new, the more profitable and the more valuable you.

WHY I WROTE THIS BOOK

Most often, people giggle and snort when they hear what I do for a living. *You teach etiquette? How did you get into that?* Well, just like any entrepreneur, I saw a need. Barely out of college, I found myself living the corporate dream. Or, so I thought. All through school, I knew I wanted to go into business. I wanted to wear a suit, carry a briefcase, go to meetings, negotiate deals, attend business dinners, go to conferences, travel and do all the "corporate" things that go along with this. What I didn't consider is the people factor. I didn't consider what it would be like to sit in a meeting and have people make decisions that were clearly self-serving. I didn't consider what it would be like to try to work with people on a project who were not willing to make compromises in their schedules in order to get the job done. I didn't consider what it would be like to watch a co-worker get drunk at a client dinner. Lastly and most impressively: I didn't consider what it would be like to see a manager or company leader become so uncomfortable in times of pressure that his performance was compromised.

Later, after opening and then closing my own business and opening another with my husband, I was very clear on what I wanted my next venture to be. I *knew* what I had seen and experienced wasn't right and it didn't have to be that way. I *knew* people could make decisions about their own conduct that could make for a better work environment, a better project execution or a better customer experience. So, after watching and learning for 15 years, I decided I could do something about this breakdown in business.

4

My hope is that this book will affect a change of heart for those in business. We are all offered a chance at success and it matters *how* we seize that opportunity. You can't force your way through life like a bull in a china shop and expect true relationships to develop. You can, however, choose to be mild-mannered and patient, kind and giving and reap the benefits of putting others before yourself.

How to Use This Book

As you know, changing habits accumulated over a lifetime can be difficult. But you also know that only through change can positive results occur. I have written *The Civilized Minute* as concepts that can be quickly absorbed and put into practice immediately to reinforce the message. The book is arranged into Daily Lessons that focus on common topics all business professionals encounter. These Daily Lessons are designed and written to be read in about a minute and provide actionable items called Savvy Suggestions you can use right away. Read one each work day of the week and you will be better equipped for the unexpected situations life throws your way every single day.

You may be tempted to read the book right through in one sitting. Go ahead! Just be sure to go back to the beginning and take in a Daily Lesson over the course of 16 weeks. Receiving the message as a regular and constant dosage greatly increases your awareness about behavior and works toward creating life changing traits that your competition will envy. Reading these concepts more than once will only improve your ability to retain them and use them.

Also, I have included a concluding section entitled From Here. Once you complete the 16 week exercise, this section will further guide you on implementing the lessons learned. Remember, just reading about these topics will not have the impact on your career – they must be implemented!

At the end of this book, I have compiled a list of Kate's Quips. These are short mantras or thoughts you can print out or jot down and refer to often. I have found that by quickly reviewing these ideas often, habits change. I hope you enjoy reading them and using them in your daily life as much as I have enjoyed writing them for you.

DAY 1

OFFICE DECORUM

When you are in an office setting, a certain level of decorum is expected. Some industries are much more relaxed than others so be smart enough to know your environment and play by those rules. The ambiance of a bank, for example, is very different than the vibe of a young and hip advertising agency. In either place, there are certain expectations that we as humans have.

> **Birthdays.** Some offices make a big deal over birthdays with decorations and practical jokes while others simply serve a cake each month. Know the plan and don't stray too far off course. While fun, birthday celebrations don't really do anything to promote your product or service, so spend your time on the relevant stuff.

> **Music.** Music is a major component of an office environment in some places and viewed as a distraction in others. Know your volume limits and abide by them.

> **Attire.** The way you dress is only one of the ways you present yourself as a professional. Likely, there

is an office dress code. Lest you want to be viewed as a bully and disrespectful to the company and your boss, follow the rules.

Food. If your desk is situated in a high-traffic area, don't eat there. Do you honestly want everyone who walks in the door to watch you try to eat Lo Mein? Don't store food in your desk. It will become old and odorous before you realize it and by then, the 'unclean' cloud is hanging over your head.

Voice control. Use your inside voice, please. It's annoying when you can't hear the person on the phone because someone is recounting last night's big game at the water cooler.

SAVVY SUGGESTION At your next performance evaluation, ask your manager to give you feedback on these topics. Your desire to improve in these areas will signal your boss that you are aware of your impact on the overall work environment and can appreciate the big picture.

DAY 2

FIRST IMPRESSIONS

Like it or not, first impressions still matter. Seven to seventeen seconds are all you get to make sure you are remembered. It helps to think about it like this: *If I only had 7 to 17 seconds to impress my ultimate customer, what would I look like and what would I say?*

Some like to argue that we aren't judged by our looks. See ya later, Success, if you buy into that. Theoretically, I agree. However, like it or lump it, that's not how it works. Show up for a job interview in a rumpled and ill-fitting suit and I guarantee you will not be chosen above the guy whose resume looks just like yours but chose his clothing wisely. Further, that whole "who you are" thing gets summed up pretty fast through your lack of attention to detail and lack of preparation in showing up for a job interview like that.

Here are the Big 3 when it comes to impression management:

1. Are you well-groomed? You must be clean and tidy. Not one person wants to smell last night's happy hour or your lunch hour workout.

2. Are your clothes clean and fitted? Don't be afraid to have something altered. Often, a minor modification can make a tremendous difference! If you find yourself saying 'No one will notice', remember to also say to yourself, 'Yes, they will'.

3. Are you confident in your appearance? If you aren't, this will show up very quickly. If you are self-conscious and shy, your eye contact will be off and you will be reluctant to engage in conversation. Figure out what is holding you back and fix it. Change your diet, go to the gym, hire a stylist to get you outfitted, just work on it. The fact that you are addressing your burden will give your confidence a lift and others will notice.

SAVVY SUGGESTION Make an appointment with a stylist who will critique and make suggestions. You want feedback from the top of your head (haircut and style) to the bottom of your feet (shoe style and condition).

DAY 3

5 CAREER MYTHS YOU NEED TO FORGET

Your career success has much to do with your frame of mind. There is no room for anything less than an energetic and inspired disposition. Below, you will find 5 myths that should be read this one time and tossed from your mind. These are destructive mindsets that can make you appear passive and irrelevant.

I've been here so long it doesn't matter. They know me. People are always willing to catch a glimpse of the less than perfect you. Be careful not to be complacent.

No one is watching. In the cafeteria, online, on your way out the door...people are always watching.

I'm stuck. You are stuck only if you choose not to see any new opportunities. You are never stuck if you keep learning.

*They won't mind if I...*take supplies home, park right here, wear this only today. If your actions are in direct conflict with company policy or are costing the business money, they mind.

I'm too old/I'm too young. Clients and managers care more about your contribution than your age.

SAVVY SUGGESTION: Carefully consider how you regard your worth. Don't short-change your contribution by letting insecurity outshine your work.

DAY 4

WHAT YOUR TABLE MANNERS SAY ABOUT YOU

Table manners are a huge part of impression and brand management in business. Not everyone thinks so, so if you take these tips to heart, you will gain the edge on your competition. Not knowing how to successfully navigate your way through a business meal suggests that your competency is narrow and lacks the well-roundedness required in today's global marketplace.

- Know how to correctly hold eating utensils. Hint: shovels and fist-grips have nothing to do with dining.

- Know how to manage the place-setting and table accessories. Bread and salad plates on the left, liquids on the right, napkin in your lap, pass salt and pepper together, and watch out for the finger bowl (it's for your fingers; you'll regret it if you drink it).

- Be aware of how you treat the servers. Your tablemates (i.e. business associates) will be quick to assume any condescending treatment of "subordinates" happens at the office, too, and that sort of behavior is considered to be in poor taste.

- Don't panic when something unexpected happens. It's just Murphy's Law that you will spill something on your tie or drag your sleeve through your salad dressing. Remember that this stuff happens to everybody – even the most sought after customer in your business. Simply clean up after yourself without fuss, make a brief apology and move along with the conversation.

- Know when to excuse yourself – verbally and literally. Say excuse me *quietly* when a burp or sneeze escapes or when you need to go to the bathroom. Don't go into detail about how your sinus infection progressed or your urgent need to use the facilities. You should leave the table to reapply lipstick (ladies), answer *only* an urgent phone call and to tend to personal hygiene emergencies (blowing your nose, removing food stuck in your teeth, etc.)

- Perfect your table manners. Learn how to eat unusual foods, how to order a bottle of wine, how to manage your napkin throughout the meal, how to eat in the Continental and American styles of dining. Pay attention to the smallest detail in your quest to perfection.

SAVVY SUGGESTION Take a course or buy a book that offers detailed instructions and illustrations for learning table manners. Then, practice at every meal.

DAY 5

BE RESTAURANT SAVVY

If you are charged with taking a customer out to dinner, what you are actually being asked to do is make sure they have a good time. Or, if you are invited to a working lunch to discuss the particulars of a deal, your task is to seal the deal. In either situation, it is in your best interest to set the stage to work to your advantage (ie make you look like the guy someone would want to do business with). Don't be confused. This is not about the food. This is about business, so do the following to avoid the avoidable.

- Know the restaurant. Be certain the food and service are the best. Don't take a client to a place you've never tried.

- Get there before your guest so you can 1) make sure the table isn't right next to the bathrooms and 2) know which chairs each of you will take so you won't do the silly table dance.

- Get your credit card to the manager before your client arrives so the bill can be taken care of without the awkward check moment when the server leaves the little folder on the table. This demonstrates major

15

initiative and that you know how to make sure things go smoothly. The client will remember that you are a person who gets things done and is considerate of others. Just don't highlight the fact that you are doing this, it defeats the purpose.

- Have a budget in mind so you can make suggestions accordingly. Simply say "The pasta dishes are delicious." or "I think I'm going to have the same chicken dish I had before. It was terrific." They should get the hint from your remarks about how to place their own order.

- If you *really* want to impress, consult with the manager and pre-order the menu. This works especially well if you are anticipating deep conversation and would like to be able to talk to your guest without interruption.

- Drink one alcoholic drink. One.

- Use your table manners. Use your table manners. Use your table manners.

SAVVY SUGGESTION These are not hard things to do, but take a practice run with a friend before you try out your new savviness on a customer. Your friend will love you. Your customer will, too.

DAY 6

THE POWER OF YOUR PRESENCE

There is power in simply being. The trick is in the *how*. Think of the most influential leader you have ever been around and you will get an idea of what I'm talking about. True leaders, those people whose natural stance and demeanor inspires strength and whose first reaction to any situation is the opposite of self-preservation, are not perfect. They make mistakes and they fumble, but they do it with maturity, integrity and judgment. These are qualities you can't list on your resume. You have to *be* them. You have to show you hold these close to your conscience by every decision you make – big or small. And, not to scare you, but they are easy to spot. The lack of these qualities is even easier to spot.

Maturity. I often hear people talk about not going to an event because they don't know who will be there. That usually means they have ignored the request for an RSVP. Don't fall victim to insecurities typically seen in young people striving to find their way.

Integrity. Doing the right thing is not something you do when the result will work in your favor. Doing the right thing should be your natural reaction. One slip up in this department will put you in the history books as a weasel and it takes years to overcome that impression.

Judgment. Having good judgment means you are able to make a fair decision based on fact and not emotion. Choosing to wear a suit, for example, is a choice you make based on fact. A suit may not be your preference, but it may be what's appropriate for the occasion.

It can be a chore to ensure your behavior mimics your character, but the rewards are well worth the effort. It's a choice you need to make prior to trying circumstances. Don't get caught in a sticky situation without knowing what your core values are and how you want to be viewed by those around you. The decision to be professional and reputable is best made when you are not full of negative emotion and can think clearly about your intended career path.

SAVVY SUGGESTION: Become part of a mastermind group so you can surround yourself with like-minded professionals. This can be a terrific support group when you need encouragement.

DAY 7

VOLUNTEER

What does volunteerism have to do with business etiquette? Discontent breeds bad behavior. Find a discontented person and I'll show you someone who likely spends way too much time focused on their own needs and wants.

I know of one company who requires each employee to perform 5 hours of volunteer work each month. Their belief is that volunteerism breeds a worldly and outward perspective that cannot be achieved any other way. Simply put, they believe that if their employees put some energy toward productive things outside the office, they will be more productive inside the office.

I believe there is another benefit here and that is this: volunteering allows you to push your boundaries of comfort. If you have never worked in a soup kitchen, you may initially feel uncomfortable there. But, it's good to force yourself into situations that require you to figure out how to cope. As adults, we tend to nestle down with our comfortable friends in our comfortable neighborhoods and go to our comfortable jobs. Challenge yourself! Get uncomfortable! That is how you learn.

During your adventures in volunteerism, you will be expected to meet new people, try out new surroundings and learn how to perform new tasks with grace and humbleness. There's no room for pride here. You are to serve with grace. That means you will use skills like looking people in the eye when you talk to them – no matter who they are. You will shake all different kinds of hands. You will make conversation with people you have little in common with. You will ask questions when you don't know how to do something. You will be friendly and smile a lot. You will be cordial and offer to help out in different ways. You will be proactive by looking for needs and trying to fill them.

Reaping the benefits of volunteerism depends on your mind-set. Choose to allow these new experiences to build your character and expand your horizons.

SAVVY SUGGESTION: Schedule volunteer opportunities throughout the year just as you would any other appointment. If it's on your calendar, you can't use the excuse that you are too busy.

DAY 8

HAVE A GOOD HANDSHAKE

Anybody in business will *tell* you it's important to have a good handshake, but how many people actually do? And, when it's bad, it's really bad. There are 2 main points to keep in mind about your handshake:

- form (are you doing it right?)

- function (are you using it right?)

Form

When you shake a person's hand, you should be standing, facing them fully (shoulders squarely in their direction), smiling and looking them in the eye. The exception to the standing rule is if you are stuck in a booth of people and it's physically impossible to stand. To pardon yourself by saying *Excuse me for not standing* is not acceptable. That just means, 'I'm too lazy to stand up for you and you really aren't that important to me.' Ouch. You may even tilt your head slightly to one side if you are particularly glad to meet someone. The grip should be firm and web-to-web (the web is the skin between the thumb and the index finger). Two or three pumps, and no slaps on the back or fraternity brother rituals! This is all business and it applies to both men and women.

Function

Bearing in mind, by nature, a woman's hand is smaller than a man's hand, men should still give a woman a firm handshake. Under no circumstances should the handshake offered a woman be the finger-grip (this is where the man grasps the woman's fingers below the knuckles). Nothing says 'You are my subordinate' more clearly. Women, by the same token, should be the first to offer a hand. Not because social etiquette makes us believe this is correct, but because it's a quick way to show initiative and resolve. Even though women have made great strides toward equality at work, not every woman *acts* like it. So, women, step to the front of the line when it's time to pass out handshakes and enjoy the sound of opening doors. You should offer a handshake when you are introduced to someone, when you first see someone and when you leave.

If you have sweaty palms, spray them lightly with unscented anti-perspirant. Works like a charm.

SAVVY SUGGESTION Ask some friends to grade your handshake for you. You may be surprised at what they say.

DAY 9

COMMUNAL SNACKS

A favorite trick of meeting organizers is to offer food. You may find a pyramid of water bottles on a side table and bowls of nibbles scattered about on the meeting table. M&Ms and jellybeans are favorites behind mints. Having something to do in addition to listening seems to hold participant's attention and make them active listeners. However, actively digging through the bowl to get the favored jellybean flavor is yuck. Before long, participants will be staring at the "digger" and not paying attention to the agenda.

As the organizer, you should plan to offer individually wrapped snacks. Place them in a bowl or basket still in the wrapper. I once found a co-worker at her desk painstakingly unwrapping Hershey's Kisses and dropping the candy in a bowl without letting them touch her fingers. She said she didn't want people to worry about germs during the meeting. I didn't have the heart to tell her only the first person to pull from the bowl would have that luxury.

As the participant, you should know the correct way to serve yourself from the communal snack bowl. Use a spoon to put a few mints/jellybeans/nuts/candy on a napkin. Then, eat from the napkin. This allows you to enjoy what is offered without touching what other people might like to eat. If there isn't a spoon, go get one from the break room without making it a big production. If there aren't napkins in the meeting room, get some paper towels when you go get the spoon. There is no need to call out the organizer's oversight. That will only serve to make you appear high-maintenance. This is also the tactic for social gatherings where snacks are served. No matter where you are, no one wants to eat what your fingers have grazed.

SAVVY SUGGESTION: If you find yourself in this snack-at-a-meeting situation and don't have the utensils you need to politely serve yourself, be the first to slyly bring in enough napkins and spoons for the entire table – without drawing attention to yourself.

DAY 10

HOW TO WRITE A THANK YOU NOTE

Writing a thank you note at all is a bonus feature in the business world, but writing it *correctly* is what separates the men from the boys. Email thank you notes are not altogether wrong. They just may not be right for every situation. The thing to remember is who will be receiving the note. An older, more traditional person, for example, may be more impressed by a handwritten note sent via snail mail than an email waiting in his inbox on Monday morning. Thank you text messages are rarely acceptable. And, remember that notes can be written for all sorts of reasons – not just when you get something wrapped up as a pretty package.

The most well-received thank you notes are:

- *Hand-written on nice card stock with your name, your monogram, your company name or your company insignia.* No preprinted messages or slits for your business card. If the card folds, the front should NOT say 'Thank You'.

- *Sent within 48 hours of the gesture.* If you have a scheduled business dinner, begin the note prior to even going. Address the envelope and leave it on your desk so you will see it immediately afterward.

- *Specific.* If you were invited by a client to play in a golf tournament sponsored by the client's company, you might say, "It was a pleasure to spend time with you and Gary in the great outdoors and to get a little exercise. You all gathered a nice crowd and run a mean tournament. Thank you for inviting me to play golf yesterday."

- *Sales pitch free:* It's fine to refer to whatever conversation took place, but don't muddle your message. The intent of this communication is not to sell; the intent is to show appreciation.

- *Genuine.* There are plenty of books that give examples of thank you notes, but likely, that's not the way you would say it. Put it in your own words because the recipient will know if you plagiarized. Who uses the word 'solicitous', anyway?

SAVVY SUGGESTION Order the right stationary and find a reason to write one note a week. It doesn't have to be in response to someone giving you something. Maybe someone has simply been nice to you!

DAY 11

HOW TO HANDLE A BUSINESS CARD

I met a man once who had terrible business card etiquette and I remember the experience vividly. When I extended my hand to introduce myself, he slapped his business card in my palm and I never got the handshake. I bet it would have been a limp fish one. And you can bet I didn't bother keeping his business card. The card exchange should happen well into a conversation and only initiated if there is real potential in a relationship developing. Don't offer your card unsolicited and don't go around asking for cards willy-nilly.

Be ready for someone to ask you for your card. You should not have to rummage through a bag or dig deep into your back pocket. Keep a stack in a case and in your breast pocket (men) or in a handy pocket in your purse or briefcase (women).

When you hand someone your card, it should be facing them so they can begin reading as soon as their eyes focus. It should be clean, not bent or crumpled on the corners and current. Don't scratch out an old email address, for example, and write in your newest one. That's sloppy and unprofessional.

When you accept someone's card, it is respectful to actually take a moment to look at it. They may want to point out a particular bit of information and if you have already stuffed it in your pocket, you will appear awkward when you have to pull it back out. Use the card as a way to keep the conversation going. You might say, *Oh, I see your office is on the east side. Has the city finished the park renovation yet?*

The business card should be viewed as an extension of a person. Treat it respectfully.

SAVVY SUGGESTION At your next networking event, pay particular attention to those who handle the business card exchange with ease. Use these tips along with their model behavior to improve your own game.

DAY 12

How To Be A Good Host At Home For Business

Having the people you work with in your home is nothing to sneeze at. They will see the *real* you. They will see what you looked like in college by the pictures on the wall, they will see how dirty you let the carpet get before you have it steamed, and they will see what kind of books you read and movies you watch in your spare time. Be prepared that some conversation may be required when your lunchtime workout partner spies your basket of knitting supplies.

When the invitation is extended, be sure to include specifics: where to park, whether spouses and children are included, attire, what they should bring (if anything), and the occasion.

Much like when you host someone in your office, your job as the host is to make sure everyone is comfortable and enjoying themselves while you are viewed in a favorable light. Know your guests, their likes and dislikes so you can anticipate their needs. If you are expecting a vegetarian, be sure to have enough veggie items on the menu so he or she won't starve. If you are expecting someone who doesn't drink, mix up a pitcher of a non-alcoholic drink to offer them. Excessive decorations and formalities may not be what is in order when you consider the culture of your business and office. Make sure to have an understanding of the environment your boss and associates are comfortable with, because if your guests are uneasy, the party will flop.

If you are hosting a big work event at your home, consider hiring a caterer to handle the food and drinks. You don't have to spend a lot of money, but you will be relieved of the burden of taking care of everything. You can then focus on your guests and the purpose of the event.

SAVVY SUGGESTION Don't get so tied up with replenishing drinks and food trays that you forget about the people. Mingle, relax (the group *will* respond to your anxiety level) and be sure to thank everyone for coming over.

DAY 13

HOW TO HANDLE CRITICISM

If someone offers you constructive criticism, take it gracefully. Getting huffy over your performance review makes you look like a child and will make your manager wonder how you would accept similar comments from a customer. The biggest favor you can do yourself is to be open to the ideas presented. Listen to another person's perspective. You probably didn't realize that eating lunch at your desk every day was a nuisance to your co-workers. In your attempt at being frugal and healthy, you may be smelling up the office for the rest of the day. It's ok that you didn't think of that. You could go outside or to the break room. Being open is being willing to compromise. While you may function best under a tight deadline, the other people on your team may prefer to hit milestones along the way so they aren't rushed at the last minute.

Be willing to try out the advice you get – you will probably learn something. And, if you learn that the new way simply does not work well for you, go back to that person and have a conversation. Your demeanor at the time the advice was put forward will dictate the tone of future conversations. If you accept a review with dignity, your request for reconsideration will be accepted with dignity. If you pull the

Diva card and reply to criticism with complaints and excuses, your manager will cringe if you bring up the topic again.

Remember, connecting with people is one key to career success, so don't alienate yourself because you think you are always right.

SAVVY SUGGESTION If you receive constructive criticism from your boss or a client, work out a schedule to address the problem. Go back to that person in a few days to let them know you appreciate their being candid and have devised a plan for improvement. Be big and be bold.

DAY 14

WHEN YOU HATE YOUR JOB

If you have never been in a job you disliked, count your lucky stars. But, when has a little dissatisfaction been a reason to wreck your entire career? If you hate your job, carry the sentiment around as if it were the combination to your own personal cash vault. Very, very carefully. It's ok that you are probably looking for another job, but don't give yourself a reason to quicken the search. As soon as management gets wind of you being unhappy, they will be keeping an eye out for a reason to let you go. Or, they will confront you about whatever rumor they have heard. No company wants a disgruntled employee on staff.

It's unlikely you can talk about the fact that you are unhappy in your current position without saying something derogatory about the company and that is inappropriate. If you have a valid grievance, take it to your manager. If something just doesn't suit you, keep quiet.

Perform your job tasks with diligence and don't fall for the ole *I'm not going to be here much longer anyway* trick. You have no idea how long it will take you to find another job. Poor job performance will raise questions from your boss that you may not be ready to answer.

It's wrong to job-hunt while you are on the clock. The internet works 24/7, so save this for after work or during your lunch break.

Be careful you don't utter one negative word online because companies view social media sites as gold mines when it comes to keeping tabs on employees.

Know you hold the key to office morale. If you start talking and grumbling about the things you dislike, you will bring down morale in a hot minute. Be responsible and mature. It's not fair to those around you who enjoy their position to be faced with having to defend it.

SAVVY SUGGESTION: This is a mind-over-matter situation so you have to decide that you will appear happy and content until the 5 o'clock whistle.

DAY 15

HOW TO PARTY WITH THE OFFICE

Office parties offer a great chance to make a great impression – or not. You can either put your best foot forward or shoot yourself in the foot, so go into party mode knowing what your objectives are. Are you there to mingle with your co-workers, build rapport, earn their respect or are you there to win the traditional game of quarters that happens late at night every year? Are you there for a chance to impress the company president and his wife or are you there for the beef tenderloin?

You *should* be considering the office party a way to promote yourself. Use these tips to make yourself comfortable, charming and absolutely fabulous:

- Attend. Don't give up the chance to hang out with your colleagues and get to know what makes them tick.

- Don't drink too much alcohol. Stories that come from drunken office party mishaps do not die quickly or quietly.

- When you get there, seek out the highest level person responsible for the gathering, shake their hand and thank them for a nice event.

- Hold your drink in your left hand. This leaves your right hand dry and ready for a handshake.

- If you are to wear a nametag, wear it on the right side of your chest.

- Don't go through the food line more than once piling your plate high. First, it looks greedy. Second, you shouldn't spend so much time on the food when you could be rubbing elbows with the new marketing manager putting together a team to evaluate a new client from Rio.

- Some people simply are not comfortable in a group social setting – even if it is a for-business function. Be sure to speak to those that look most uncomfortable. Your initiative will be noticed by higher-ups and you can be certain the favor won't be lost on your co-worker. This is the sort of act that will come back to you twofold.

SAVVY SUGGESTION Practice these tips at purely social events so you will be ready when office party time rolls around.

DAY 16

HOW TO BE UNEMPLOYED GRACEFULLY

It stinks to be out of work, but most everybody has been there. You may have the tendency to think since you don't have a job, you don't have to think about things like image and good behavior. That is wrong and can put you front and center with an opportunity lost if you think that way.

During a time of unemployment is when you should be on top of your game. You should be introducing yourself to everybody you run across and using the time to hone certain skills that can put you ahead of the next person you interview against. That means you actually do have a job. Your job is to find a job. So, who will hire you if you show up at the softball game looking wrinkled and unshaven? Need to run to the newspaper stand? Take 30 seconds to tuck in your shirt and brush your hair.

Show composure and confidence. When you are around friends and they are complaining about their busy schedule or heavy workload, words may linger on the tip of your tongue like *At least you have a job* or *Must be nice.* Don't be snide. Listen carefully to the conversation. You may find an opening to inquire about within their company or with a company they are talking about. Your mind and attitude has to be open to any possibility. If you are busy being bitter, you will miss it. If you become unlikeable, no one will recommend you, either.

Keep up your image. Make sure you at least *look* like a person someone would want to hire. Skipping showers and allowing your hair to have a permanent cap ring is not your ticket to the top.

Keep learning and don't spend too much time alone. Go to classes and seminars where you will be surrounded by people who value learning. This will keep your mind engaged and your demeanor friendly. Too much alone time and you will forget how to engage those around you.

SAVVY SUGGESTION: If you are unemployed, keep a daily log of your activities so you can make sure you are staying productive.

DAY 17

IN THE PARKING LOT

Do you think maintaining your business persona can wait until you get inside the building? It can't. Coworkers and superiors alike find your choices in the parking lot equally as telling as what you do inside the office.

If you are the first to take the parking space in front of the door every morning, no one will likely offer you a piece of quickly disappearing cake someone left in the break room. They will assume you have already taken care of yourself. If you crank up your car at 5:00 each afternoon with Vanilla Ice blaring, you probably won't be chosen to work with a hip and young new client. If you sport an ego-bearing vanity tag that says MRMAN, you can be pretty sure you aren't viewed as Oliver Herford's muse when he said "Modesty; the gentle art of enhancing your charm by pretending not to be aware of it." There really is no need to speed through the parking lot, either, Mario.

I worked with a lady once who taught aerobics after work. When most people were leaving the building and milling through the parking lot, she could be seen changing out of her suit and into her spandex in her car. Literally, she could be seen. I often wondered if she thought her windows were tinted or if she secretly wanted to put on that show. Sitting in a room with her, I had to make a conscious effort to forget the parking lot exhibition and focus on the meeting agenda. She was very astute, but that show created a major distraction.

SAVVY SUGGESTION: Put on your game face the last couple of minutes before getting to the parking lot. Don't wait until you get to your desk.

DAY 18

AND GUEST

It is pretty common to be invited to an event hosted by your company, a client or a vendor and encouraged to bring someone along. This deserves careful and deliberate consideration. You will be judged and remembered by the guest you bring. Your best let-loose-and-blow-it-out friend may not be the best choice for an awards banquet. And, your new can't-keep-my-hands-off-you partner may not work out for the 10 year anniversary picnic.

Consider the type of event on the books and think about who would fit comfortably in that setting. If you are unsure about a candidate, ask them about it. If they tell you they don't like events like you describe, don't try to convince them to go anyway. You want to take someone with you who will be relaxed and not intimidated by the people or surroundings.

Be fair to your guest by telling them everything you know. Time and place are easy to remember to share, but tell them about the people that will be there, the reason for the event, how they are expected to dress, if there will be food and/or drink. Everybody operates best with the most information, so tell it all.

Make sure you are clear on the relationship between you and your guest. Naturally, you will introduce your...what? Girlfriend? Buddy? Pal? Partner?... to people you work for and with. Introductions should go smoothly and not hold any surprises.

SAVVY SUGGESTION: When it's time to find a friend to escort you to a business function, choose carefully. Make sure you are taking someone who will make you look good and make others in attendance glad you came.

DAY 19

CUBICLE COURTESIES

Nearly every person who has ever had the pleasure of calling a cubicle home can talk about things their neighbors did (or didn't do) that drove them to distraction. Here are the things you should consider if you spend your days in Cubeville.

1. <u>Volume</u>: The volume of your radio, podcast, webinar, desk phone ringer and your voice can be a major distraction for those around you, so keep it down.

2. <u>Smells</u>: If you *must* eat something really smelly for lunch at your desk, at least take the trash to the break room so your neighbors don't have to smell it all afternoon. Further, be aware of how much cologne or perfume you use. Don't make it too much of a good thing.

3. <u>Movement</u>: Slamming your file drawers and cabinet doors shakes the walls and desk of your neighbor. Be gentle.

4. <u>Speakerphones</u>: Don't use one if you are in a cubicle. Use a headset instead to free up your hands.

5. Meetings: Schedule a meeting room or someone's office to hold a meeting. If you try to do it in your cube, you won't have enough room and will disturb others.

6. When you are away: Turn off anything that makes a noise.

7. Personal conversations: Don't force your personal problems on those around you. Make personal calls and hold conversations about personal matters in private.

8. Privacy: It's easy to forget your coworker's cube is their office, so notice if they appear too busy to be interrupted. *Do you have a minute?* is a good way to determine if they mind your interruption.

9. Your stuff: Be mindful of the impression the items on your desk and tacked on your cube walls give. Make sure your plants aren't growing out of control, there isn't any trash sitting around and cobwebs haven't been spun between company artifacts. Be neat, tidy and don't hang pictures of yourself looking or acting any differently than you would look or act in the office.

10. Passive-aggression: If your cube neighbor tends to leave his desk for hours on end and his phone rings off the hook driving you crazy, talk to him rather than unplugging his phone every time he steps away. Retaliating won't help. Simply ask him to forward his phone to voicemail or turn off the ringer.

SAVVY SUGGESTION: You know the things your cube neighbor does to make you crazy? Make sure you aren't doing them also.

DAY 20

HOW TO MAKE SMALL TALK

You've heard there is an art to being able to make conversation. That's true, but it can be learned. There is no need to run into a meeting the millisecond before it starts because you are uncomfortable sitting around the table while people shoot the breeze around you. If the topics tend to be gossipy and catty, you are correct to avoid them. But, if you simply don't know what to say, here are some tips you can use for anything from downtime at the office to cocktail parties:

- Make a mental list of conversation starters that will suit most occasions. Avoid the weather.

- Don't start with an observation about a person's appearance unless it's stellar. *Wow, look at your new haircut!* is a don't. A vague remark like this is open to interpretation. *Love the suit - makes me want to spruce up.* is better. Just be genuine.

- Read something other than company material. Create a list of media outlets and blogs (www.alltop.com is a good blog directory and www.ted.com is a good website you should use for this) that will give you fodder for conversation. This will keep you well-read and make you conversational with most anyone. Stick to larger publications that report on human interest stories. Small, local outlets tend to only print who is doing what.

- Know where you are going and who you will see, then prepare. If your boss asks you to represent him at an art gallery opening, read up on the artist and the venue. It's ok to call the organizer to ask who will be attending so you can have their names in your head. The organizer will be pleased to hear you want to be prepared since that will only work to make the function a success.

- Begin with *Tell me....* This forces a more elaborate answer than Yes or No. *Tell me about how you prepared for such an energetic presentation* leads to a better conversation than *Did you have to prepare a lot for your presentation?*

- Don't begin with "I heard...". This makes you appear gossipy.

SAVVY SUGGESTION Force yourself to strike up a conversation with someone you don't know once a day to keep in practice and try out your own strategies.

DAY 21

HOW TO BE A GOOD HOST IN YOUR OFFICE

When you have invited one person or a group of people to your office for a meeting, to watch a presentation or for a day-long work session, your primary objective as the host is to avoid the avoidable. *Anticipate anything that might make the meeting or relationship derail and put a fix in place before it happens.*

If you know this client is especially eco-conscious, offer recycling bins for water bottles and soda cans. If you know the bathrooms are difficult to find, announce their location prior to the start of the meeting. You want to make the event of being in your domain pleasant and enjoyable. Imagine the thoughts a client may have if they leave your office after having a bad experience. They would not be too impressed if your cell phone seemed to ring every time you introduced him to someone or if the temperature had been unbearably hot. While these may seem like details that don't matter much when you are talking about a multi-million dollar deal, it's the influence these small details have on your relationship with your customer that matter. And believe me, *the devil's in the details.*

If you host a meeting on a day when rain is pouring down, everyone arrives wet and windblown and you offer nothing to make them more comfortable, the thing that will stick in their minds long after the meeting is over will be the fact that they were wet and windblown – not the presentation you worked weeks to perfect. But, let's say you recognize 30 minutes before the start of the meeting that the rain is coming, so you dig up a stack of towels for drying off and offer hot tea when they arrive. *Now*, they will not only remember being wet and windblown, but they will also remember the effort you put forth to make them comfortable. *You showed them that business is also about the people.* That level of consideration is translatable in business - it puts you on the fast track to gaining trust and that catapults you toward big deals.

SAVVY SUGGESTION One hour prior to your client/boss arriving, think of one thing you can do to show you are being considerate of their time and effort. Put it in place before they arrive.

DAY 22

WATCH YOUR WORDS

Don't you know someone whose everyday, anywhere language is foul? They can turn a very benign topic into a sexual reference in under 3 seconds and turn "Have a nice day" into an after midnight Comedy Channel routine. Why do they do that? Do they really think they are that funny? Maybe they feel like they have to try that hard to be one of the guys. Well, guess what? Nobody's impressed.

Business is not about being cool, anyway. It's about the product and service you provide. What does language have to do with that? Nothing, unless it's offensive. Language should be a means to an end, so don't turn it into an opportunity to blow a developing relationship. You may think it's ok to fall into that tough guy or girl routine because your client drops the f-bomb in every other sentence. *That's just the way we talk* you may think. Wrong. Stay away from nicknames that sound condescending, too. 'Sport', 'Doll', or 'Dude' only make you look immature.

So, what do you do if you are in a group who is spouting off obscenities? Leave. Simple as that. You don't want to be considered guilty by association nor do you want to be viewed as one who condones your coworker's ranting. It is not your duty, however, to save their wretched souls. Management will address them if their language gets out of hand, so there is no need to wag your finger and attempt to correct anyone.

This is one of those areas that will set you apart from the crowd. Remain articulate rather than colorful. That is what sends the message that you are steady, long-lasting, credible and confident.

SAVVY SUGGESTION Notice how people react should you choose to be colorful. If they glance around, they are checking the crowd to see if there is someone you have offended. If using certain words is part of your natural speech, work to eliminate one offender each week.

DAY 23

WHEN YOU CAN'T GET BEYOND THE INTERVIEW

It's a common frustration. *You* thought the interview went well. You talked a lot. They nodded. Your resume rocked. They put it in a folder. So, *why* aren't they calling back???

Maybe it's not the resume or your new interview suit or the fact that you got there precisely 10 minutes early. Maybe it's <u>you</u>. Maybe you are sending signals that are making it difficult for companies to believe you would have their best interest at heart and represent their brand flawlessly. Run through this list of deal breakers and make sure you aren't shooting yourself in the foot.

- <u>When people talk, do you listen?</u> People can tell if you are simply giving them face time and your body language will give you away on this one. You can't keep glancing beyond the interviewer's shoulder every time someone walks by the door and still appear that you are genuinely interested in what's happening in the here and now.

- <u>Do you walk your own talk?</u> Do you talk about approachability and friendliness yet get short with the interviewer if he fails to bring your resume to the meeting? If so, you are sending mixed signals. Interviewers take every encounter with you and apply it to a business situation to help them decide if they want to jump in bed – figuratively speaking, of course.

- **Do you have another personality online?** Talking smack online and giving off a foreign bravado will catch up with you. Everyone Googles and sites like Facebook and Twitter pay a lot of money to make sure their results show up on the first page.

- **Do you look like a professional or a chump?** Take a good long look at yourself in the mirror before you leave for an interview. If you are rumpled and slovenly, you will have to work double-hard to let your interviewers know that you are detail oriented, a self-starter and motivated towards greatness. It doesn't have to be a suit, but it does have to fit perfectly and be clean.

- **Do you know who you're talking to?** Be aware of who is listening to you during the interview. If your counterparts are 50 or 60 years old, cut back on the 20-something vernacular.

SAVVY SUGGESTION: After each interview, debrief with a trusted mentor. Review the questions and your answers, your attire, and your resume. Be ready to work on areas that need improvement.

DAY 24

WHEN YOU ARE NERVOUS

Everybody gets nervous. If someone should tell you they don't ever get nervous, they are lying. It's even ok to be nervous. Being anxious means you are aware of your impact on a certain situation. The recognition that you play a role in producing a desired outcome should drive you to overcome those feelings. Listen to your own reactions regarding your environment and feed off that energy. Make this an internal exercise, though, because being visibly uneasy will make others question your expertise and worthiness.

Your physical presence can express more to those around you than your words. You can tell someone you aren't nervous, but the glisten on your upper lip may say otherwise. Likewise, you can tell an interviewer you are experienced in sales, but if you fidget in your seat during the discussion, they are going to wonder just how many times you have actually had a conversation with a potential customer. A seasoned professional, they will think, would not be so uncomfortable while they talk about their work history.

Take note of these common nervous gestures and work to keep them at bay:

- **Fidgeting**. You may be bouncing your leg or tapping your fingertips on the table and not even realize it.

- **Avoiding eye contact**. Maintaining eye contact is imperative for you to appear confident.

- **Touching your hair**. This is a habit you may have developed and not know it. Women tend to put their hair behind their ears while men run their fingers through their hair.

- **Gesturing with your hands**. Moderate use of your hands during conversation is good. Wildly waving your arms about is not good.

- **Closing your body**. Crossing your arms over your chest, sitting in a chair angled away from the action, even clasping your hands in front of you can be subtle obstructions when trying to connect with someone.

SAVVY SUGGESTION: Create a mock interview or meeting environment with a trusted friend. Video this exercise so you can critique your body language.

DAY 25

PRESENTING YOUR PERSONAL SPACE

With every job comes a work space. Whether you work at home or in an office across town, you have a designated space where you do your thing. Your personal space is viewed as an extension of how you work. If your desk is cluttered with papers and files, people will assume you are unorganized in your approach to your job as well. It may be "organized clutter" to you, but it doesn't matter what *you* think. It matters what *they* think. Honestly, would you seek out a guy whose cube smells like yesterday's Thai lunch when you have something pressing that must be done right and fast? How about the person whose desk is full of stacks? Stacks of papers, tangles of cords, piles of takeout menus, and the ever-present-over-flowing trashcan? It just looks dirty. Will that person be asked to entertain clients? Likely not when you can't be sure she won't drag along that trail of disgust.

It's great to have pictures, diplomas and meaningful or inspiring trinkets, just make sure everything is arranged in a neat and tidy fashion. If you have a picture, put it in a frame. If you have a plant, discard it if it dies. Think moderation. Less is more.

You've probably heard this quote by Albert Einstein: If a cluttered desk signs a cluttered mind, of what, then, is an empty desk a sign?

Don't fall for it. You are not Albert Einstein.

SAVVY SUGGESTION Walk away from your work space. When you come back, imagine you are seeing the work area for the first time. What impression did you have? Now consider what you should change, throw away, organize, or re-arrange.

DAY 26

KNOW HOW TO SAY NO

Having nice manners does not mean you are a pushover. Just the opposite, actually. Mastering business etiquette allows you to have all sorts of ways to say *You have got to be kidding! There is no way I'm doing that!* without hurting feelings or leaving the impression you are not a team player.

Here's how to gracefully decline just about anything:

In order to remain in good graces, you must decline with grace. That means your reaction to any request must remain emotionless. No exclamations about the absurdity of what is being requested. Watch your facial expressions. Don't furrow your brow or frown.

Don't ramble, instead be direct. Let's say you have been asked to organize the monthly birthday lunch for the 3rd straight time and you are ready to let someone else take the lead. Simply say, *Thank you for asking again, but I'm going to decline. I'm on a deadline.* There is no need to talk about why you shouldn't have to do this every single month and how everyone complains about the same ole cake, anyway. Smile, look the person directly in the eye, give him your answer, and you are done.

Decline quickly. Unless you honestly need to mull it over or check your calendar, decline the request right away. If you are perceived to be unsure or easily swayed, more and more people will ask you to take on whatever they don't want to do themselves.

Set the stage. If you stay busy at the office and don't spend a lot of time around the water cooler, people will assume you are too busy to even be asked to coach the company sponsored little league team. This will allow you to seek out the "extra" things that fit your schedule and personality.

SAVVY SUGGESTION Think ahead to a proposition you already know you will decline. Create your response and practice it in front of a mirror until you can say it with ease.

DAY 27

KEEP YOUR COOL

There are lots of ways to describe it: blow a gasket, come unglued, blow up, have a meltdown. They all mean the same thing. They all mean that some trigger caused you to put down all sense of decorum and act in a most unacceptable manner. Think Steve Martin in *Father of the Bride* when he went off the track in the grocery store because hotdogs were sold in packs of 8 and buns were sold in packs of 6.

Here's the bottom line on this: you can't afford to lose your cool anywhere or anytime.

Everybody has their own set of stresses so don't feel like the Lone Ranger or Mr. Big Shot on this. And, everybody is expected to deal with them in such a way that doesn't inconvenience or bother anybody else. While I'm sure the guy who took the last bit of coffee from the machine just before you is compassionate about your alarm not going off this morning, your ranting at him isn't going to make him run down the street to get you a latte. In other words, your actions in a fit of frustration simply will not change anything. Except this...

If people view you as a hothead and one who can't control his emotions, guess who will not be invited to be on a team leading a new and time sensitive project? No one wants to work with somebody who can't work under pressure and remain cool. Every breath you breathe and step you take at work should be to further your company and your career. Shouting at your teammates during a company softball game does not do that.

SAVVY SUGGESTION: Figure out a technique that will get you centered (taking a walk, deep breathing, etc.) and commit it to your existence. Something that can be done throughout the course of your workday would be best.

DAY 28

COMPANY GYM ETIQUETTE

If your company has a gym dedicated to its employees, you will only find people in your organization there. That means you can't completely let your business etiquette guard down. Naturally, you will change out of your work clothes and into workout gear, you'll sweat and you may even grunt, but you still must mind your professional manners.

- Don't try to talk shop with someone while they are on the treadmill or under the bench press machine.

- Put a little effort into how you are dressed. Don't wear t-shirts with inappropriate slogans or wording and don't wear clothes that are too revealing.

- Your gym behavior is an indicator of your office behavior so pick up after yourself unless you want to be viewed as careless and self-serving.

- Follow the gym rules about equipment placement and signup sheets.

- Don't stare. I'm sure it's amazing to see Paula in spandex, but keep yourself together.

- Don't be the expert. Not everyone wants to hear how you would do it.

- Bring a sweat towel to wipe down the machines after you finish.

- Show some modesty in the locker room. Remember, you will see these people again.

- Don't use your workouts as an excuse to be late to an appointment or to miss a deadline.

SAVVY SUGGESTION: If you have workout habits that do not support your professional image, go to a gym other than the one that offers your coworkers a front row seat.

DAY 29

EYE CONTACT

It seems like anybody with any sort of job would have already mastered the skill of good eye contact. But, take a look around you. How often do you run into someone in your professional life who has terrible eye contact? They may glance in the direction of your forehead, but do they really hold your gaze? Or, do they stare at you relentlessly? Likely, you do several things for yourself to appear poised, educated and confident. All of this can be made moot if you don't have appropriate eye contact.

To appear most professional, maintain your gaze on the other person's eyes or forehead. Don't let your eyes drop below the nose because it is distracting to the other person. Haven't you talked with someone who only looked at your mouth? It makes me think there must be something in my teeth and I certainly can't concentrate on what I'm saying.

The more social gaze rests between the person's eyes and mouth. If you are in a place with loud background noise, you may need to watch the person's mouth to lip-read. That's ok, just don't make it a habit and as soon as they are finished speaking, your eyes should go back to their eyes while you respond.

For your eyes to drop below the chin is inappropriate in business. This is an eye signal that may be misinterpreted as a sexual advance and that's never good for your career.

Holding direct eye contact should happen for about 80% of the time. Less than that and you appear shy or like you are hiding something or, worse, incompetent. More than that makes you look creepy.

SAVVY SUGGESTION Identify in your head one conversation during which you will pay particular attention to your eye contact. Grade yourself. Now, identify a person whose savoir-faire you admire and grade their eye contact. How did you compare? If you need to improve, practice on the television. News channels are the best because the anchor's face usually fills up the screen. Force yourself to look the anchor in the eye for 10 seconds. When you have mastered that, add 5 seconds. Do this until you are ready to work your new skill out in the world.

DAY 30

PERSONAL STUFF

The events in your personal life do not have anything to do with your job tasks. Further, those in your business life, aren't overly interested in what's happening in your personal life. If your dog had puppies or your hairdresser moved your appointment yet again, it's not really what *everybody* wants to hear about. When you run into a co-worker in the break room, put your conversation skills in play without focusing on yourself or your life. It's unprofessional to engage – and by 'engage', I mean 'corner' – everyone you see between the copy room and your desk with tales of your personal struggles. Your teenage daughter's boyfriend's mother is not typically a topic of grave concern at the office.

Spending several minutes throughout the day talking about non-work related topics sends the message that your job is not your top priority. It's ok and right that your kids or your aging parents or your volunteer work are more important to you than your work responsibilities; however, if you are going to enjoy success in your career, you must give the impression that work is No. 1 on your mind during the workday. Work-life balance is key to any happy and satisfied person's existence, so understand this: I am talking about impression management. You want your boss and your customers to have faith in your readiness to get the job done. If they have to interrupt your story about your neighborhood watch meeting last night to find out if the meeting you scheduled is still on track to begin in 15 minutes, you aren't sending the right message.

SAVVY SUGGESTION When you develop your own list of conversation starters, make sure you aren't getting too personal. No sob stories and less is more. Try to go through an entire conversation using the words 'I' or 'my' only 3 times.

DAY 31

FLIRTING AT THE OFFICE

Don't confuse "building rapport" with flirting. Even if your company doesn't have a problem with nepotism, office flirting makes you appear immature and ill-equipped for the job. It will look as if you have other priorities than tomorrow's deadline. You want your boss to be certain that when it's time to woo a potential client away from the competition, you are ready for the task. If there is any concern whatsoever about how the job will get done, you will be passed over. There is no way the company will risk an HR disaster and bad press over you. It's likely you aren't *that* valuable.

Flirting also introduces a certain tone in a group or office that owners and managers hate. Suddenly, there is so much chatter about the come-hither glances and accidental meetings in the parking lot that customer service begins to suffer. Imagine your 5th grade teacher saying, "Pay attention and get finished with your work so we can continue." That's what your boss is thinking. He's thinking you are holding up progress by creating commotion over something so *not* business-related. The guy who was hired about the same time as you, however, is smiling in his briefcase at the harm you are doing your career and the help you are doing his.

To be called out for flirting is to be doused in fluorescent paint. Management will watch you like a hawk because if a "victim" comes forward with complaints about your advances, you become very expensive to have around. It's a strategic and financial decision to fire you should an HR situation arise and your credentials won't matter a bit.

SAVVY SUGGESTION If someone is flirting with you at work, you can either ignore it wholeheartedly or have a pointed conversation about how you intend to spend your time while on the job.

DAY 32

NOT SHARING

Not telling everything you know is as good as lying. You may not have considered the full impact of not sharing every piece of information, so let me explain it.

Scenario: One job duty of Elizabeth, the receptionist at Company ABC, is to take phone messages for the company president, Mr. Smith. On Tuesday morning, she had an extra long phone conversation with her sister while at work. During her personal call, she noticed a persistent caller on line 2 but chose not to answer the call believing if it's really important, they will call back. Two hours later, Mr. Smith came out of his office asking if he had any messages. Elizabeth replied, "No". What Elizabeth had no way of knowing is that Mr. Smith was waiting on a very important phone call from his banker to confirm funds had been shifted so that the company could pay its employees that very day. Had she mentioned the calls that came in but went unanswered, Mr. Smith could have called the bank himself.

From Elizabeth's perspective, it may seem like a minute detail that doesn't really matter. Elizabeth's perspective, however, isn't very broad. Don't be an Elizabeth. Realize that you do not know all the workings of a company or project therefore do not actually know what is important and what's not. It is important that you share every piece of information with your boss or your team. If you think the information will reflect negatively on you, that's no reason to jeopardize the greater mission. Contrary to what you may think, you will leave a better impression if you "throw yourself under the bus" for the good of all. Being able to think globally and selflessly is an attractive attribute in business.

SAVVY SUGGESTION: At the end of your workday, review your actions. Were there times you could have handed over helpful information but chose to withhold it? It's not too late to offer it up. Think big and be bold.

DAY 33

HOW TO INTRODUCE YOURSELF

Nothing, and I mean nothing, says *I've got it going on* like knowing how to present yourself to another person. The facial expression, the eye contact, the posture, the handshake, the words – they all work together to send the unmistakable message that you are tasteful and a force to be reckoned with. You could run into someone dressed in drag and still leave the impression that you have class and tact if you make this routine second nature to your very existence.

Here's how it's done:

Facial Expression: Your facial expression should be relaxed and pleasant. If someone startles you by turning up in an unexpected place, don't screw up your face like you smell something bad. Maybe you feel some pressure because you can't recall their name. Don't panic, just smile and say, "I know I know you. Would you tell me your name again?"

Eye Contact: Your eyes should be looking directly into the eyes of the person you are meeting. They should *not* be darting around behind that person scouting for a *better* person to meet.

Posture: By standing tall and straight, you are sending the message that you are confident in yourself and interested in them. A slouchy stance implies that you really aren't too concerned with what's happening in the here and now.

Handshake: This is the most important component of any sort of introduction. You must have a good handshake. If you perfect all other things but have a bad handshake, they will only remember the bad handshake.

Words: Imagine walking up to someone, putting out your hand, looking them in the eye and saying, *Hey. I'm Kate.* Usually, that awkward silence kicks in pretty fast and you walk away wondering what they were thinking. Now, imagine walking up to someone, putting out your hand and saying, *Hello, I'm Kate Lewis. I am a friend of Susan Smith's. We met last year at her spring picnic. It's nice to see you again.* Now, they're going to be thinking some good stuff: they will think you have a good memory, they will appreciate your coming up to them because they were probably thinking you looked familiar, and they will think you are a go-getter because you showed initiative (even though they can't see that stack of procrastination on your desk). Be sure to introduce yourself with your first and last name – always and every time – and follow with a good conversation starter.

SAVVY SUGGESTION Create your own little introduction speech and routine now, before you need it. Just keep it genuine to your personality. Create it, practice it and memorize it.

DAY 34

BEHAVIOR FOR ONE AND ALL

It's disheartening to see a co-worker who you thought was a "nice guy" act in a condescending way towards his wife. Or, to see the company president ignore the doorman's assistance when the CFO idles up for a chat. Someone is always watching and WILL catch you acting like a turkey.

The way you behave toward one – no matter who that "one" is – is the way you should behave toward all. It's very telling about a person's character if they are curt towards the waitstaff at a restaurant. The impression given is that person has a sense of entitlement and not everyone enjoys the level of attention he does. Gag. We are all just people who do a job for a living.

Acting impolitely toward certain people (namely, those who provide you some sort of service – trash man, postal carrier, school teachers, servers, etc.) does 2 things:

1. It takes the focus off your work and puts it on you. People will begin to associate your name with your behavior and not your work.

2. It makes people question your character and motives. Personally, I don't want to go on a business trip with

someone who I know is rude because I would curl up and die if he acted bad towards the potential customers we were to court. AND, how do I know he wouldn't throw me under the bus if the situation got sticky?

SAVVY SUGGESTION Hire a business coach to shadow you for a period of time. A trained professional can give you unbiased guidance on your demeanor, choice of words and actions that may make you appear condescending and rude.

DAY 35

Got A Problem?

You must have a very big thorn in your side if you plan to go to management with a complaint. Know this before you start your dissertation on the lack of diplomacy in the office: The moment your comments are determined to be of the negative sort, you are tagged as a complainer. Not all is lost, however, because redemption comes nearly immediately when you begin to offer well thought out solutions for the grievances you bring. Think solution, not problem. Your boss does not want to hear you complain and whine, but he doesn't mind hearing you point out an opportunity for greater productivity.

The way you deliver your comments also matters, so break down your beef into these 4 sections:

- **The Problem**: First, make sure whatever makes you unhappy is actually based on a true office shortcoming and creates an obstacle when you try to do your job. The way Cal pops his gum may make it hard for you to concentrate, but that's not justification for a new policy banning gum in the office. Second, be able to articulate the problem and its effects clearly. Don't include phrases that allude to emotion such as *It drives me crazy when...* or *Everybody hates it because...*

- **The Solution**: Spend some time thinking through different solutions to the problem. It may help to type up some notes before your meeting. You want to make sure your boss knows that you are thinking clearly and for the benefit of the business.

- **The Presentation**: Walk confidently into the meeting with your head held high. Be proud! You may have just discovered a gap and found a resolution that could have bottom line results. Speak with assurance, not quietly and timidly. Take your notes into the meeting in a clean binder. Don't appear as if you just threw some things together.

- **Afterward**: Be prepared that your suggestions may not be implemented. Don't be discouraged and certainly don't sulk and tell your coworkers what a jerk your boss is. There may be other changes in the works you don't know about. You can rest assured, however, your professional approach and initiative didn't go unnoticed.

SAVVY SUGGESTION: Got a problem at work? Look again. That actually could be an opportunity. Come up with a solution and work your professional magic when you present it to your boss.

DAY 36

HOW TO ENTER A ROOM

When you are in a room (restaurant, bar, conference room, etc.), where do your eyes typically fall? On the door because you want to see who is coming in. So, it's important to enter a room with confidence and flair. It's that first impression thing again.

If you are entering a meeting room, have your trappings together and secure before you darken the door. You should not blow through the door with papers flying and cords dragging. It looks sloppy and unorganized and people will immediately think the same of your work.

When you enter, take a step to the right so you don't block the door and stand tall with good posture. It's ok to stand there briefly to get your bearings - figure out where you should sit, who you should speak to before you sit down, etc. Make good eye contact with those already there, have a pleasant expression on your face and shake hands with those immediately around you. This deliberate and thought-out approach to an everyday activity will pay big dividends in the long run. You are giving the impression that you think before you leap. It also shows a tremendous level of confidence. You are confident and authoritative enough to simply stand without fidgeting, working to impress or having a buddy. Not many people can do that.

SAVVY SUGGESTION *Rushing* into a room may be habitual for you. Practice in places outside of work, like a coffee shop, until it feels natural.

DAY 37

WHAT NOT TO SAY

Honestly, there are some things that should never come out of your mouth when you are with people from work. Ever. It doesn't matter if you have been doing business with a vendor for 20 years and he knew you "when", there is still a level of professionalism that you *must* keep up in order to stay on the fast track. In most situations, hurt feelings could be avoided if the offender would think before they speak. The first words that come to mind upon meeting the boss's wife for the first time may not be your most eloquent.

This is not a complete list of things not to say, but these are the biggies:

- How old are you?

- How far along are you?

- Is she your wife? Is he your husband?

- How much did that cost?

- Did you hear about...{anything or anybody local when it's derogatory}?

- Are you mad that you didn't get chosen?

- How was your evaluation?

- How much do they pay you to do that?

- Is that real?

- Anything related to bathroom humor or bodily functions

I have seen people say things similar to any of those listed above simply in an effort to make small talk or to be funny. It always ends badly. There are some topics that are none of your business or that no one wants to talk about, no matter how well you know someone. Even if your intentions are good, the fallout will not be. Think before you speak.

SAVVY SUGGESTION: Don't react. When you are with work folks, your actions and words should serve to make you appear intelligent, tactful and observant.

DAY 38

CELL PHONE TACTICS

Just like me, I'm sure you consider your cell phone to be indispensable. It can also be the most uncomplimentary tool in your toolbox. There are very specific pitfalls that come with this particular technological jewel and here they are:

- If you wear your cell on your belt, take it off. The look smacks at a 'fanny pack' and that never looks good on anybody.

- If your cell has bling, undo it. It makes you appear superficial and materialistic.

- If you have to stop someone from talking before you answer a call, don't answer it. Voicemail and text exist for a reason, so let them do their jobs and you do yours – which is to not offend a customer or demean a co-worker by answering your cell when they are mid-sentence.

- If you have something in your mouth when your phone rings, don't answer. Are you seriously going to crunch and smack into someone's ear when it could be THE call that seals THE deal?

- If you must type, don't do it while you are talking. Multi-tasking is a necessary skill these days, but there is no way you can give your full attention to the person on the phone if you are typing an email to someone else.

- If you really want to appear genuine on the phone, use your facial expressions as you would if the person were right in front of you. This will give your end of the conversation a friendly and purposeful tone.

- If you anticipate background noise, don't dial. That means you may need to wait until you are off the street, out of the store or off the subway before making the call.

- If you are going into a meeting or a meal, put it on Silent, not Vibrate. Everyone knows what the vibrating sound is and it, too, can be distracting or annoying.

- Don't use the ring-back tone feature if you use your cell for any business purpose whatsoever. It's unprofessional. Plus, you will never be able to choose the perfect song to leave the perfect impression.

SAVVY SUGGESTION When your cell rings or when you are ready to place a call, think. Think about this list and get a fast read on whether it's ok to go ahead with the call or if it would be better to let it go to voicemail.

DAY 39

HOW TO ATTEND A MEETING

Yes, there *is* meeting etiquette and if you have attended a meeting or two in your day, you would probably like to tack this up on the office bulletin board. Typically, meetings are seen as a waste of time because, often times, they are run so inefficiently. Something that should take 30 minutes and is advertised as such ends up taking a full hour. Yet, in defense of the organizer, only so much can be accomplished when the Goon Squad gathers in one room. So, master this list of meeting etiquette so you can get in and out and on with things.

- <u>Know why you were invited</u>. It's unbearably frustrating for someone to show up and not know the topic up for discussion. If you don't know why you are there, you aren't prepared and the meeting may as well be called off. Ask for the agenda. It won't appear pushy, and it will demonstrate that you value your time and the time of your coworkers.

- <u>Get there on time</u>. Duh.

- Don't bring your lunch and make everyone see, hear and smell your spaghetti. It's distracting and off-putting, to say the least.

- Speak up. If you have input, offer it up. It could be something that alters the path of the entire project. If you wait until afterward to email your thoughts to the leader because you were too timid to say it out loud, you've wasted a whole bunch of time.

- Be mindful of table space. No need to bring a notebook, your PDA *and* your laptop – that must be plugged in. Choose one method to capture your notes and any action items that you will follow-up on.

- Don't talk over someone or speak in a condescending way. The lack of common courtesy will bring down the tone and productivity level of the entire room. Remember that you are but one of many needed to get the job done.

- Mind your posture. Don't slouch. Sit upright with your forearms rested on the table or by your side. This says 'I'm here, I'm prepared and I'm ready for action.'

SAVVY SUGGESTION In your next meeting, choose a seat where you can observe the entire room. Take in body language, reactions to comments and suggestions, notice who looks like a winner and who is clearly a Goon. Guide yourself accordingly and don't be like the Goon.

DAY 40

How To Participate In Team Building Exercises

A lot of people snicker and roll their eyes when it comes to team building exercises. They immediately start telling stories about certain things people did to show off or that resulted in them embarrassing themselves. They are also quick to criticize the event itself by saying things like "I can't believe we had to go to that park when it was so hot that day" or "I don't get how some ropes and a piece of wood are going to make me a better worker."

If you subscribe to this way of thinking, you are simply one of a thousand people just like you. In other words, you don't get it. Management spends a good bit of time and money preparing for these outings and it's disrespectful and unappreciative to sound off about the details that don't suit you.

Do not sulk around the office and make snide remarks in the days leading up to the exercises. Your boss will hear about the grumbling and you will be tagged as a trouble-maker for disrupting something that is designed to benefit the people *and* the business. It's unappealing to company higher-ups for you to express viewpoints that clearly display your inability to see the greater picture. When the day arrives, be careful your competitive spirit doesn't get in the way of good clean fun. Yelling and screaming at your team during competition will definitely be a downer for everyone. The following day, be sure to give a verbal 'thank-you' to the organizer and/or your boss. Expressing appreciation for something most people complain about shows company spirit and insight into what it takes to be successful.

SAVVY SUGGESTION Buck up, participate with a smile on your face and try to learn something.

DAY 41

OVERNIGHT BUSINESS TRAVEL

For the young and zealous, a business trip evokes a sense of adventure because you are leaving home. For the seasoned executive, a business trip means even more time out of the office. Both sentiments can cause you to be lackadaisical towards the whole affair and complacency is your enemy. Preparation is the basis for a successful business trip.

Don't count on everything to work as it should, because it rarely does AND the client you are visiting is only interested in output, not the trouble you had to go through to make something happen. Pick up your dry cleaning at least 2 days before leaving to allow for any mishaps with your laundry. The rumpled traveling salesman look is way out of style and makes you look like the trip was an afterthought. Arrive at the airport in plenty of time to get through security. Missing your flight and using the "hard time getting through security" excuse is also outdated. Make sure your bag weighs in within the airline limits so you don't hold up the group. If you are traveling with companions, be considerate. Offer to help with the group's luggage, offer to exchange seats on the plane with someone who would be more comfortable in your seat. If you are stuck waiting on a flight, offer around your newspaper or IPOD. If your director is traveling with you, kill time on the plane doing something that speaks to your competence. When you get to the hotel, don't rush ahead to be the first at the registration desk. Unless you have a true sense of urgency, just chill. When it's time to eat out, be sure to dress accordingly (warmer climate does not mean you should wear a tank top) and don't order the most expensive item on the menu because it's on the company's dime. In other words, be pleasant.

Unexpected things are bound to happen, so be ready with your tools, not your temper. Anything from lost luggage to mixed up hotel reservations can tempt the lesser sort toward bad behavior. Remember, how you handle these unforeseen circumstances is a direct reflection on how you would behave if the situation were strictly business. And, your travel companions are taking notes. If you believe "what goes on the road, stays on the road" is true, you haven't looked at Twitter.

> **SAVVY SUGGESTION** Make a checklist of things to do and things to pack for a business trip. Also, tuck away a few clothing essentials and toiletries for business travel only so you will always be prepared. Act as if everyone on the trip knows your mother. And remember, this is business, not a vacation.

DAY 42

WHATCHA DRINKING?

In the business world, alcohol should be considered the devil's candy. Things that happen during that second and third glass end up on places like Facebook and that's never good.

Rule: One drink. And, one drink is good. You can show off your wine tasting savvy or impress your Scotch-drinking boss with a nice selection from the top shelf. Use the drink as a conversation starter. One drink allows you to show finesse. More than one drink allows you to show off more than you should.

Everybody has a story in their closet related to over-indulging. That's just life. But, you are a grown-up now, so you must show some discipline and pace yourself. The magic in not over-drinking is that you will walk away with the goods on everybody in attendance. It's your ace in the hole. Ever wonder why two of your co-workers can't get along? Wait it out while they have a couple of drinks and you'll probably get to see some old wounds open up. Ever wonder why another co-worker is never asked to travel for the company? You might see that while he works well in the office, he is a social misfit. These moments of inhibition and vulnerability that rise from the bottom of a bottle give you the information you need to become indispensible to your boss. Showing your competence in and out of the office puts you on the fast track to success. The next day, while others are nursing regrets, they will wonder if and when you will ever screw up. The answer? Never.

If you do not drink, remember to not make a big deal of others' decision to partake. Drinking is a personal choice, and no one appreciates someone judging them on their decisions. If someone asks why you don't drink, just casually mention that it is just a personal decision. You don't have to go into details about why, and most people will simply accept that you don't drink and move on.

SAVVY SUGGESTION At a work-related social event where alcohol is served, sip your drink to make it last longer. When your glass is finally drained and you don't want to be empty-handed, order water or something that looks like a drink to avoid unwanted questioning about your choices (that's not the time or place to get into your position on professional decorum or how they will have to face the music tomorrow while you will be grinning like a Cheshire cat). Be social, not preachy and, certainly, do not be drunk.

DAY 43

HOW TO BE INTRODUCED

When you are being introduced to another person, the 7 to 17 seconds it takes for that person to record a first impression of you starts the moment all 3 parties make eye contact. That means, while the person is making the introduction, you shouldn't be caught looking around the room for your date or your buddy or the bar. You should be looking at both people – in the eye – and your face and body language should reflect what is being said.

Let's say your co-worker is introducing you to your new boss who has just moved into the department. Maybe it would go something like, *Mr. Bob Jones, this is Mr. Mark Davis. He is our go-to guy for the mid-west accounts and is sure to be a good resource for you as you get acclimated.* Now, you are being praised, so bowing up and nodding a 'yes' wouldn't be appropriate. This is your new boss. You want to appear competent and humble, not prideful. You should be smiling and have modesty on the tip of your tongue. *John is just trying to butter me up before our tennis match, but I'll be happy to support you in any way I can.*

Catching the person's name and using it throughout the conversation will make them feel valued. When you meet a potential customer, you want to leave such a favorable impression that they are quick to remember you when you call on them later. Don't get flustered if you suddenly forget the name or become unsure (*did he say Jay or Jack??*), just ask. *I'm really sorry I'm so bad with names, did you say Jay or Jack?* Truthfully, have you ever been offended when someone asked for your name?

If you are at an event where food and drink is served, pay attention to what's in your hands when the introduction starts. Don't try to eat chips and dip and shake hands at the same time. It's awkward and someone will end up getting food on their shoes. It's best to keep your drink in your left hand so you won't offer anyone a cold and wet handshake and put your plate down until the introduction is over.

If you are at an outdoor event, take off yours sunglasses when you are being introduced. When people can see your eyes, they know you are listening and interested in what's being said. After the introduction is over and you have moved on to small talk, you can put your sunglasses back on.

SAVVY SUGGESTION When you are going to a business/social or networking event, plan ahead. Know your conversation starters, eat beforehand so you aren't caught with your mouth full and practice remembering names. Remember: you only get 7 – 17 seconds.

DAY 44

ECO-ETIQUETTE

There is tremendous value in being eco-friendly at the office. Besides reducing your carbon footprint, working toward a common goal alongside your coworkers is a terrific morale booster for the entire group. It's also a way to show you are a team player and are willing to do things that are good for everyone, not just yourself.

Take the following opportunities to be the green leader in your office:

- If you need to wash your hands, dry them with the blower rather than paper towels.

- When applicable, use hand sanitizer rather than water.

- Recycle – you aren't *that* busy.

- At an office party, offer to bring the plates and napkins. Bring products made from recycled materials.

- Seek out ways your office can become more green. Suggest them to your manager.

- Turn the lights off if you are the last to leave a meeting room, supply closet or bathroom.

- Cut old reports or papers into squares to use as scratch paper.

- Organize an office carpool.

- Use the stairs rather than the elevator.

- Select locally grown organic foods to serve at parties.

- Email meeting materials rather than making copies for everyone.

- Set your computer to go to sleep when you become idle.

- Don't print a document in order to file it in your drawer. If you can recapture the information online, don't print it.

SAVVY SUGGESTION: Being the office green leader is not an excuse to act uppity about it. Don't preach it, just be the example.

DAY 45

CELL PHONE EARPIECE

A lady told me once that she found it aggravating to walk in a store and have none of the salespeople speak to her or offer to help her. During our conversation, I learned that when she shopped, she liked to wear her cell phone earpiece. Aha! Of course, no one approached you, I said, because they assume you are already having a conversation. A few weeks later, I was hired to do some training for a management group because they were "in a rut", they said. They were hearing complaints from their staff that the office environment had become stuffy and rigid and they had even lost a valued employee to their competition. Interestingly, very early on the first day of training for this company, I overheard some conversation among the managers about the cost of the new earpieces they would be getting soon. It turned out that each manager in this company was issued an earpiece to wear at the office to help them remain "functional" during a phone call. These managers were unwittingly setting a certain tone in their office that most found miserable.

When you have an earpiece attached to you, it's like carrying a big sign that says *I am unavailable.* What message could be worse for a manager to send all day long every day of the week? It's essential that you remain open to those at work –

manager or not. No one will approach you to offer so much as a Good Morning without the reasonable expectation that you will respond back. It's awkward to speak to someone and have them respond by mouthing, *I'm on the phone.*

SAVVY SUGGESTION: Even the President doesn't wear an earpiece while he's at work. Take it off when you are in the office.

DAY 46

MYTHS OF MULTI-TASKING

One of the great trials of our day and age is to keep up. You have to keep up with the changes in technology, keep up with your running program, keep up with the plans for your high school reunion and the list goes on. In an effort to stay in the game, people are taking multi-tasking to new heights. But, it's not always good. In fact, some multi-tasking attempts end up being counter-productive with regard to your image and professional persona.

Here are the myths of multi-tasking that will hurt, not help, your productivity and your career.

- <u>No one will notice if I check/send this text/email during the meeting.</u> It's incredibly frustrating to attempt to direct a comment or question toward someone who is engrossed in their phone. If the meeting time isn't convenient, say so. Don't sit at the table and not participate.

- <u>Go ahead, I'm listening.</u> Continuing to work while someone is talking to you will not get you on the office Most Likeable list. Giving someone your attention while they speak is a small courtesy everyone can afford. Ironically, the person will likely not take so long to tell you something if you look at them while they are talking because you can give them non-verbal cues that you get what they are saying.

- **I'll just take this quick call.** That usually means the call has to do with a work issue so you feel that you can't let it go to voicemail. However, conducting business in a public place is completely inappropriate and unprofessional. Your client, boss or vendor would much rather you call them back in 5 minutes than discuss company business in the café around the corner.

SAVVY SUGGESTION: Work toward giving your full attention, consideration and respect to the people in your immediate vicinity. If you are approached during a critical time, ask the person for 2 minutes so you can get to a stopping point.

DAY 47

ATTITUDE INDICATORS

Recently, I made an early morning appointment for a pedicure. When I arrived at the salon, I was greeted by a young lady wearing sunglasses with her lips stuck way out and clearly preoccupied with her phone. She gave me a half smile and asked for my name. I'm just guessing she either was not a morning person or hated her job. I had intended to talk to her about putting a package together for a client who was interested in beefing up her image, but I decided against it. I was afraid that sending my client to this salon would reflect negatively on *me*. What if my client was greeted in the same way?

As you go about your business, you are sending all sorts of signals about your attitude. Here are the more common ways others grade your approachability.

- **The way you sit at your desk**. If you are a multi-tasking machine who spends the day frantically clacking on your keyboard with your phone to your ear, you are not giving people in your literal surroundings a chance to participate. Be aware of how many hours during the day you put up boundaries.

- **Your tone of voice**. If you are gruff and abrupt, people will assume you are either too stressed to talk or too uninterested to care. Ladies should notice if their voice is too soft. This makes you appear unsure.

- **The way you sit in a meeting**. If you want people to seek out your input, don't spend the meeting leaning back in your chair and pushed slightly away from the table. Sit at a meeting table like you would sit at the dinner table. Sit up straight and rest your arms either in your lap or on the table.

- **The tone of your emails**. It may be quicker to respond to an email with as few words as possible, but imagine how you would react to receiving the same? Read your emails before you click Send to make sure you aren't sending an unintended message.

SAVVY SUGGESTION: Ask your manager or a trusted work friend how you stack up regarding the above 4 items. Do you need to make some changes?

DAY 48

PROMOTION TIME

Finally! You are being promoted to the job you know you were meant to have. You will be able to have a say in project timelines, client assignments, even cube assignments. And, it's about time, right? I mean, who works harder than you? Who spends more time sucking up to the boss than you do? Who always gets stuck with the squeaky wheel customers? Who gets called on the weekends every single time? You! This was a long time coming, right? W-R-O-N-G.

If you are being granted a promotion and all you can think is *About time!*, you need to change your mindset and do it quick. You are a half step away from gloating and that is too unattractive to talk about. In order to be successful in any position, you must operate with an element of gratefulness. No man is an island, Superman, so be glad your hard work was recognized by someone who could give you this opportunity. You should be thinking of ways to inspire the troops and lead the way toward success for one and all, not the look on your college friend's face when he sees your LinkedIn update.

If your promotion involves new digs, don't ask for help carrying your boxes from your cube to your new office. Wait until after hours to make the change. Don't announce your new title to someone by starting a conversation with *Did you hear?* It sounds much more important when it comes from someone else's mouth. If you find there is dissention among the group because you were chosen over someone else, let some time pass before making any comment. It is likely the issue will resolve itself when they see what a fair and motivating leader you are. If the dissention does not go away, have a private conversation with each person. Do not, however, add to the rumor mill by making snarky remarks to anyone.

SAVVY SUGGESTION: Go under the radar at promotion time. Be excited about the change with family and friends and be modest and unassuming at the office.

DAY 49

STYLISH RETREAT

Transitioning from one job to another is a natural part of professional growth. Transitioning without burning any bridges, however, it what turns a little job or company change into a step up. Exiting a company with ease is as important as entering one with ease. Why? Because you need to be able to include the time spent at any job on your resume without hesitation *and* you need to be able to depend on relationships built during your time there.

Your last days on the job will be remembered more clearly than your first. Leave a favorable lasting impression because you will likely need references for whatever new job you have your sights on. Plus, it's just the nice way to go about it.

Follow these guidelines when you are in the throes of a job change:

- Work your little fingers to the bone right up to the minute you carry that last box out the door. Particularly, if the ending is bitter. Don't give anyone a reason to roast you.

- Don't badmouth the company, your boss or your coworkers. If you have grievances, you have probably held your tongue for a while already. What purpose would it serve to slam them all over town?

- People who hear about your pending change will ask you pointed questions like *Why are you leaving? Did the boss finally push you out? Are you going to another job that pays more?* These type questions are crass and uncool. Don't answer them unless your response has nothing to do with the company or its people. Ok answer: My wife got a job in Hawaii, so we are moving in 3 weeks. Not ok answer: I'm getting out of here because they don't pay me enough for all the hours I work.

- Don't let bad etiquette creep in. Arrive on time and stay until quitting time, attend office get-togethers and treat company property just as respectfully as you did on Day One. In other words, don't quit until you are supposed to quit.

- You will likely be invited to an exit interview where you will be asked why you are leaving the company. Decide before the interview begins if you want to take the risk of brutal honesty. Your career may be better served if you simply offer benign comments and suggestions.

SAVVY SUGGESTION: Very shortly after you make the decision to turn in your resignation, think through every scenario in which you will be required to make a comment. Prepare your remarks so you won't be caught off guard by the office busybody or an impromptu exit interview.

DAY 50

SMELLS

I knew a guy in high school who smelled like Dial soap. I can't remember his name. I sort of remember what he looked like. I don't remember where he went after graduation. But, I remember that he smelled like Dial soap. Smelling like Dial isn't bad at all, but I bet he would rather I remember something about him other than that.

Giving people a reason to remember you is high on the list of what to do when you want to leave a lasting impression. Having them remember your smell, however, is not the reason you should be striving for. Assess your own level of risk as it pertains to each smelly source.

Cologne/Perfume

Men and women can be guilty of wearing a touch too much cologne or perfume. Dabbing a little here or spraying a little there is not bad as long as you do it one hour before you encounter anyone. That ensures the smell won't be overpowering.

Lunch or Dinner Destination

There is a barbeque joint in Columbus, Georgia called the Smokey Pig. The food is really good but its patrons leave *smelling* like a smokey pig. If you know you will be hopping from meeting room to meeting room during the afternoon, choose a lunch place that won't leave you smelling to high heaven by 3:00.

Gym

People can smell your sweat, even if you can't. Don't think you can skip showering during the winter months. Allow enough time to cool down and clean up before heading back to civilization.

Your Breath

Choose your lunch or dinner menu carefully if you will be in close quarters with anyone afterward. Keep mints handy, but don't chew gum. Bad breath has been known to be a deal breaker.

SAVVY SUGGESTION: Look ahead at your schedule for the day. Make sure you are equipped to handle any smelly situation that should arise.

DAY 51

How To Be The Office Intern

If you find yourself in the position of an intern, you should remember that you are being evaluated at every turn. If you have long-term career aspirations with this company or any other, you can't afford to relax on any of the following business etiquette points.

- Have meaningful conversations. Offer more of your insights and opinions than you ordinarily would (without being overbearing). The people in this company are trying to get to know you, so let them see what makes you tick. Even if they don't hire you, they will be a referral.

- Do the odd jobs that others avoid. Wipe the counters in the break room, offer to pick up coffee for the group, be the first to volunteer to organize the softball team. These are easy ways to show initiative and your willingness to be a team player.

- Dress the part. Not the part of the intern, but the part you *want* to play. Remember, every time you walk in a room, you are being evaluated.

- <u>Monitor</u> your career very quietly. Don't use the company computer to check your gmail account for a response to the 50 resumes you sent out last week. Don't check your cellphone throughout the day. It's ok to have feelers out in the job market, but you must appear committed to the internship if you want a permanent position or a glowing recommendation. Also, it's wrong to use company time and resources for personal reasons.

- <u>Office politics</u>? Stay away. You are there for a specified period of time, so stay focused. Rise above the grumbling by not participating.

<u>SAVVY SUGGESTION</u>: Make a list of characteristics that would make up the too-good-to-be-true office intern. Commit to being the shining example of two-thirds of them.

DAY 52

HOW TO MAKE A GOOD INTRODUCTION

Being able to introduce two people with confidence and authority keeps you in control of the situation. This is one chance you get to appear as the leader, so show off a little by adding pizzaz and flair. I'm not suggesting cartwheels, but with heartfelt words and genuine desire to help people broaden their circle, you will earn respect by those around you.

Rule of thumb: The most important person is presented the least important person.

Example: *Mr. President, I would like to introduce Mr. Secretary.* Or, a more common way of saying it, *Mr. President, this is Mr. Secretary.* (Hint: speak the most important person's name first.)

You will also want to offer a tidbit of information so a conversation will easily follow. You might say, *Mr. President, this is Mr. Secretary. He just moved here from Florida.* Or, *Mr. Jones, this is Mr. Smith, our new sales manager. He is a gourmet chef. Mr. President offered a cooking class to our sales team last year and it was a hit.*

The goal of a good introduction is to make yourself *look* good and the other people *feel* good. If you stumble through the names, an awkward moment is sure to follow and not much conversation will come from that. And, if you really are trying to score some points by introducing your boss to someone he wants to meet, you aren't going to come off looking very favorable if you sound like a school kid – likely, he won't come to you for anything else. So, you are going to need to practice your own little introduction speech. Practice makes perfect on this, really! No one is going to walk away thinking, "Man, that guy makes a jam-up introduction" but they will leave feeling comfortable with you and the person you introduced them to because it flowed and you made it easy for them. Bottom line: You made them feel good. That kind of 'feel good' leads to trust, which leads to business.

It's also important to note that introductions often occur during the time a first impression is being made. It is well worth your time to work this into your repertoire of talents.

> **SAVVY SUGGESTION** Get in front of a mirror once a day and practice an introduction. Do it until the words flow freely and your body language appears natural.

DAY 53

TAKE A HINT

One of the most common flaws in the personality of someone who is not socially adept is that they do not easily pick up on body language and non-verbal cues. People rely on these, however, to send messages we do not say out loud using words. Being able to pick up on these cues keeps you approachable and likeable, which are important in building business relationships.

Take a look at this list to make sure you aren't missing any signs:

- Notice a person's stance when they approach you. If their weight is on one side and they are leaning one way or the other, they do not intend to stay long. Tell them what they need to know or listen to a quick instruction and let them go. Do not try to engage in a longer conversation.

- If a person wants to talk with you at length, they will face you full on – head, shoulders, hips and feet will be facing you.

- If you are having a conversation with someone and they move back from you, do not step forward in order to remain close. If the person moved away from you, they have a reason. It doesn't matter what the reason is, just give them the space they need.

- If you see the one person you need to speak to as they are walking through the door with coffee in hand and coat still on, don't approach yet. Give them a few minutes to settle in before you move in.

- If you approach a person at their desk and they don't look away from their monitor or turn their chair in your direction, it's not a good time to talk. Rather than pushing through the conversation by talking fast, ask for a good time to come back.

- Don't try to talk business in the gym, the bathroom, or the cafeteria. You will not get their full attention.

SAVVY SUGGESTION: If the people you work with seem to continuously frustrate you, take a look at the signals you are giving off. Is your body language saying one thing while your mind is saying another?

DAY 54

THE COMPANY YOU KEEP

Roddy White, Atlanta Falcons wide receiver, learned in 2009 that the people you hang around can define you and your earnings potential. While the stipulation was not written out in his $50 million contract, the club owners required him to break ties with some of his hometown buddies in order to secure the guaranteed $18 million. This came shortly after the Michael Vick debacle, so the owners were fearful that White's friends would lead him into situations that would reflect negatively on the entire team.

This is not unique to the sport of football or to an industry that is comfortable with 6 and 7 figure salaries. That's how it goes when you have people in addition to the company's owners who represent the brand. The stakeholders get anxious that outside forces will tarnish what they have worked hard to create. You were not hired as part of a package, so make sure you remain in complete control of your destiny.

You will be much better served to spend your downtime with people who bring out the best in you and push you toward relationships and activities that will enhance your worth - not put it at risk. Granted, it is tempting to stick with what you know and jump on Easy Street, but that's not where you will gain anything.

Be known as someone who works hard and keeps his eye on the ball. Not the guy who is just one of the boys.

SAVVY SUGGESTION: Take a hard look at your closest circle of friends. Do they challenge you to keep your nose clean and your head on straight? If not, create some distance and find new ways to spend your downtime. Pick up a new hobby, travel or simply ask someone new to eat lunch with you.

DAY 55

GRAMMAR AND ARTICULATION

"I know you believe you understand what you think I said, but I'm not sure you realize that what you heard is not what I meant."

Robert McCoskey

Confusing, huh? So is having a conversation with someone who doesn't speak clearly.

If you do not clearly enunciate your words and use correct grammar, people will assume you are uneducated, ill-equipped to perform most job tasks, and that you don't know what you are talking about. You don't have to walk into an interview or a group brainstorm session with the highest GPA or the most on the job experience, you just have to *appear* to be the leader of the pack. One of the ways you can accomplish this is by sounding the part.

Did you find our office ok using the directions in the packet?

Yeah, I did sounds adolescent. *I did, thank you. That is a really nice drive across the river* sounds more like a grownup and someone you might like to have a nice chat with.

Communication superstars:

- **Have a firm grasp on the English language**. They know the difference between euphemism and euthanasia.

- **Have great timing**. They do not talk over other people and don't finish other people's sentences.

- **Articulate every word**. My name is Kate Lewis, not Kay Lewis.

- **Paid attention when they were taught to diagram sentences**. They speak in complete sentences and express complete thoughts.

- **Know how to spell**. This ensures they don't mispronounce words.

Some people speak softly or even mumble because they are insecure about something. Perhaps they are unhappy with their teeth or they speak with a lisp. Try not to let vanity come between you and the next conversation that could open the door to something wonderful.

SAVVY SUGGESTION: Speech pathologists can work with you on everything from tone to facial expression. Call an English professor at a local college or university for materials to help brush up on common grammatical errors.

DAY 56

BE HEALTHY

It's no big shocker to hear that your health can impact your job performance. It was long ago that companies began to offer access to onsite gyms, healthy living seminars or even health insurance cost breaks for those who exercised regularly or didn't smoke. But, did you know that healthy living also impacts your behavior? A healthy body makes you happier, more productive, and more open-minded. This, in turn, makes you a nicer person.

I had a colleague once who worked in the IT area assigned to my department. He was the person we called when our computers acted up, so he was in a customer service position of sorts. When someone called to open a problem ticket, he was often curt and rude. It was as much a frustration to deal with his attitude as it was to deal with the computer problem. In addition to his unpleasant disposition, he was also extremely overweight. I noticed he often struggled to walk from the elevator to his desk. As time went on, he began to lose weight. I don't know what sort of exercise or diet plan he was on, but I can tell you that he became a more pleasant person to be around. He was more patient and conversational and even began to offer help before we could ask for it.

It stands to reason that feeling good on the inside allows for a better disposition on the outside. Exercising regularly and eating wisely allows you to:

1. handle stress better

2. concentrate more easily

3. increase your stamina

4. feel more confident about yourself

5. be proud of your appearance

These 5 things contribute to a productive and successful person. And, productive and successful people enjoy long-lasting careers.

SAVVY SUGGESTION: Create a plan for yourself that will allow you to make healthy changes in your life over the next year. Consider enlisting help from a nutritionist and/or a trainer so you will be sure to set attainable goals. Having a plan is only the first step, but it's a big one.

DAY 57

DON'T GET TOO COMFY

Finding yourself comfortable in your position, with your boss and with your customers is good. But, too much of a good thing can end up being bad. There is a fine line between making your vendors feel at ease enough around you to ask about the happenings in your company and gossiping about the new guy in shipping. You want to be able to grab a bite of lunch with your boss without feeling stressed, but you don't want to ever be caught without enough cash to cover your share.

Unfortunately, there are no hard and fast rules to ensure you don't appear too uptight or too relaxed. You have to use discretion and do what makes sense. Probably the biggest challenge is to *remember* to notice things like body language when you are with someone you know very well. When a level of comfort sets in, you naturally let your guard down and that's when missteps can occur.

You never want a client or coworker to feel you have forgotten the nature of your relationship. That means you must always display the appropriate amount of respect. If you don't have time to go out for lunch, I would not suggest asking your boss to run out to get a sandwich for you.

Certainly, if there is an offer, it's ok to accept, but don't confuse your manager for your errand boy.

SAVVY SUGGESTION: Think of one thing you can do for each of your clients or vendors that will re-affirm their decision to do business with you. Be specific about your appreciation.

DAY 58

THINGS YOU JUST HAVE TO GET OVER

There are lots of things in this world that you simply cannot do anything about. You can stomp and pout all you like; however, the seasons will still change and the earth will still turn. Thankfully, people who are smarter than you and me come along and create new things and processes that let us consider ourselves higher mammals. It's this introduction of something new and different that seems to get a lot of people jacked up. But, why? Why let your knee-jerk reaction to something you may not be comfortable with make you appear backwards and unbending? Show those around you how contemporary, free-thinking and willing to accommodate you can be by jumping on board the following bandwagons.

- **Different office software**. I know it's a frustration to have to change your habits with little preparation or instruction, but be open to the improvement. Look for ways you can build in efficiencies using the new tool.

- **New management**. Don't you want to move up and on to better and brighter things? Then, don't begrudge another person doing just that.

- **New policies**. Companies make changes as the economic and market environment change. Be glad someone is keeping an eye on the big picture for you. That long-term outlook will keep you employed.

- **Cross-training**. It's the new office norm. Companies are becoming better managers of their resources by cross-training their teams rather than hiring someone every time the wind blows. Rather than thinking 'that's not what I was hired to do', think how glad you are to still have a job.

It's ok that you don't know how to do something when one of these changes comes about. Just don't use it as an excuse. Verbalize your questions, not your complaints because the latter only makes management wonder if you can keep up.

SAVVY SUGGESTION: When a situation arises that you wish weren't happening, do not digest it out loud. If it is something out of your control, decide how (not if) you will embrace it.

DAY 59

IT'S THE LITTLE THINGS

My name is Kate Lewis, and I double-dip. I will admit, however, to knowing about a man who went on a job interview, was taken to lunch at a Mexican restaurant and didn't get the job because he double-dipped. I guess I like to live on the edge.

Double dipping is a really small thing that makes me feel good. There are also really small things that make me feel bad...or mad...or even a little postal. Ironically, it seems the small things can get us the most riled. In fact, my husband would rather I wreck our car than double-dip.

I have compiled a list of the most common office gripes I hear from those I train. Have a look:

Not cleaning up after yourself. If you do not wipe away the water ring your lunch cup left on the counter, it's going to make someone pretty mad when they put their folder on top of it.

Not doing your share. If everyone is to pitch in to answer the phone while the receptionist is away, try picking up the phone every now and then.

Going out for a smoke and not exhaling all the way before you come back inside. Doing so makes you smell horrible.

Arriving late and leaving early. It's irritating for you to act like the rules don't apply to you.

Being a bully. Seriously, how old are you?

Implying to customers and vendors that you are the head dog. Maybe one day, but it's not today.

If you are guilty of any of these, it's really too bad. You probably have no idea how you are disliked.

SAVVY SUGGESTION: On nearly any given day, you can hear people at work griping about something. Listen carefully. If they are talking about something you do and your response is *Well, I wouldn't if...* stop right there. The fact that you are doing it and creating office turmoil is reason enough to stop.

DAY 60

HOW TO OFFER CONSTRUCTIVE CRITICISM

First, you cannot offer criticism in a productive manner if you are feeling at all emotional. The element that makes the conversation constructive is for the comments to be purely factual and have nothing emotional behind them.

Let's say you asked your assistant to work up a spreadsheet showing the birthdays of everyone in the office and you asked for it to be complete by the end of the day on Tuesday. Wednesday at lunch, she comes to you with a list of people, last name first, and in alphabetical order.

Incorrect response: *Little late, huh? I needed this for a meeting this morning. Why did you list the names with the last names first? I know everyone by their first names, not their last. Oh, and don't you think it would be better to put this in birth date order so I don't have to pick through the list to find the July birthdays? Go do it again.*

When you have to fire her for tweeting *My obnoxious boss thinks I can read his mind,* know that she's right. You can't expect anyone to give you things you have not clearly and specifically asked for, so these elements of the assignment are not up for critique. Probably, the response was abrupt because she returned the task after the time you asked for it. As a leader, you have to be able to separate your frustration from the facts, otherwise, you will not be able to lead effectively.

Better response: *Both of us goofed up on this one. I failed to mention I wanted the names listed in birth date order and you failed to provide this to me on time. Let's both do it again. I need this by 4:00 today. Can you do that?* Eye contact should be solid but your tone should be light. You should be completely focused on the subject and not distracted by your cell or email.

Constructive criticism is not pointing out all the shortcomings of a person or their performance. It is finding why someone didn't perform up to snuff or a project didn't pass muster. Sometimes, that means the leader must admit fault or the subject must admit a failing. In either case, you must remain open to suggestion and conversation and have the very best interest of your subject at heart.

SAVVY SUGGESTION: One full day after offering constructive criticism to someone, ask them for feedback. Did they find your comments beneficial? Did they feel you were bullying them? Listen carefully to what they say and consider their remarks.

DAY 61

GENDER JUDGMENT

Should you pull out the conference room chair for your female coworker? Should you hold the elevator door for a man? Is it ok for a female to suggest an after work drink with a male team member to further discuss a project?

I knew a lady once who had a big chip on her shoulder because she was a female. She wore her hair cut very short – and not in the cute pixie style. She wore suits that bordered on manly. Her tone of voice was even slightly deeper than the average woman – and I'm not sure that wasn't intentional. And, her conversation was often about "the men" like they were tribal or something.

I knew a man once who had a big chip on his shoulder because he was *not* of the female persuasion. When a lengthy and complicated project timeline was announced, he turned to me and said, "You probably don't care about this since you'll probably just get pregnant so you can be out when implementation gets here."

I currently find myself in the company of a male who can't seem to *forget* that I'm a female. When we are gathering for a meeting, he sits down with a chair in between us. He calls everyone in the group by their first name, except me...I am Mrs. Lewis. As the group gathers, he shakes everyone's hand except mine...to me, he bows.

Do you see the recurring theme of immaturity here? Expressing any concern whatsoever over gender is archaic and closed-minded. If you expect to find value in only the people that are just like you, you will be met with disappointment over and over again. Look beyond the gender and enjoy the person.

Yes, it's ok for a female to offer to discuss something over a drink after work – only if that fits the culture of the group. If she asks in a coy manner, she's not thinking about work and if he starts breathing faster as 5:00 nears, neither is he. Chairs and doors are not held nor offered because of gender. They are offered as a matter of courtesy. If a female meets a male at a door and he has his hands full, she should open the door for him. It's not a come-on, she's just being nice.

SAVVY SUGGESTION: If you have preconceived notions about coworkers based on their gender, grow up. Otherwise, HR will come calling and that will not turn out in your favor.

DAY 62

GROOMING

If you have been through my training (or read the introduction to this book), you have heard me refer to poor social skills as the silent killer of your career because once you reach adulthood, people are reluctant to offer suggestions on very personal matters such as attitude, choice of clothing, demeanor, or... your lack of grooming.

This is an area that can challenge your self-discipline abilities, but few areas of business etiquette are more important. If you are not properly groomed, it makes people feel uncomfortable. People who are uncomfortable around you will not seek you out for any reason – not to play in a pick-up basketball game, not to meet for brunch on Sunday and certainly not to work a business deal or interview for a job opening. You have to be willing to look at yourself with a discerning eye because it's easy to overlook things you see every day (scuffed up shoes, for example).

Read through the following areas that are typically not given due attention by men and women but can make you appear lazy, dirty, sloppy and unkempt:

- **Hair**. If you do not get your hair trimmed on a regular basis, you should. You are missing out on an entire level of cleanliness by not having a professional inspect your head consistently. If you have flakes or dandruff, don't be ashamed. Simply use the appropriate shampoo. Just be sure to address the problem.

- **Fingernails**. You don't have to get a manicure to have clean and trimmed fingernails. If your hobby involves dirt and oil, find some magical solution to get cleaned up before work on Monday morning.

- **Eyebrows**. Lean in close to your bathroom mirror where the light is good. Now, trim. Men and women alike should have short and shaped eyebrows. Salons and barber shops can help with this, so not knowing how to do it yourself is not a good reason to have scraggly hair reaching into your line of vision.

- **Clothes and shoes**. If your salary will not allow you to buy expensive items or keep up with the latest styles, you can still make certain you are not objectionable. With an iron and a lint roller, you can at least be pressed and tidy. With a shoe shine kit, you can at least appear to care about your appearance. There is no excuse for filth.

When someone is lacking in the grooming department, it is awfully hard to separate their appearance from their work. Would you want to borrow a pen pulled from a head full of messy, dirty hair?

> SAVVY SUGGESTION: Use your calendar to schedule grooming appointments that will cover all the areas mentioned here. Yes, they are that important.

DAY 63

SOCIAL MEDIA

Have you ever *said* something to someone and wish you could take it back? But, there are no take back's, unfortunately. It's out there and the person you offended can't unhear what you said. Have you ever *done* something to someone and wish you hadn't? Actions are harder to forget than words because we store visual images alongside the sounds and smells and that package lodges firmly in our memory.

Social media sites are very cool when you want to connect with someone whose experience and wisdom can work to expand your own horizons. Social media sites are also very quick and easy tools that can help you to do something stupid.

Here are some actual posts from various social networking sites:

Glad the day is over. What a waste of time.

Training class @ work. Boring!

At work on my boss's computer lol...gettin paid to be on fb! anyways hope everyone has a great day...glad tomorrow is FRIDAY

Time to play 'spot the coworker wearing the same thing as yesterday'

If you haven't heard of anyone being Facebook Fired, then you are living in a cave. Seriously, why would anyone post these things for any and all to see? At a minimum, it makes you look like a complainer, but even worse, it could be proven that you are stealing time (money!) from the company by not working during working hours. Management loves sites like Twitter, YouTube, Digg and even Foursquare because it allows them to see the *real* you without having to tap your phone line or hire a private detective.

> **SAVVY SUGGESTION**: Use social media sites to one up your competition by learning new things and expanding your network. If you need to vent, call up a friend and don't type away your frustration. If you feel most tempted while on the clock, don't even open the application.

DAY 64

BE ORGANIZED

Not too many people can claim that organization comes naturally to them. Admittedly, it takes a lot of work to keep your desk, your calendar and your files organized. And, for most of us, there are parts of our work life that are strictly virtual while a good part of our personal life has not yet made the leap into the virtual world. It can be maddening to try to keep track of important dates and times that are sent via snail mail to your home address along with the ones that come only to your work inbox along with the invitations that sit in your Facebook notifications. You would think some grace would be allowed when you are 20 minutes late for a meeting, but that's not the case. Nor are you cut any slack when you arrive without the mockup for the new ad campaign sent via email 3 days ago.

Organization is so elusive to some that there are people who have built their entire professions around teaching it. Professional organizers are quick to tell you about the negative impacts clutter can have on your day. And stacks of items to be dealt with? Nope. Not good at all. But there is another point to consider. What kind of performer do people assume you to be when you struggle to keep up with your tasks or even your cellphone?

Teams are assembled and companies hire employees because no one person can do everything. So, if you are employed, it is because someone needs you to complete certain tasks and they have to be confident you will do just that. If you are not employed, it is imperative that you appear equipped and assembled and ready to fill a need. Whatever the magnitude of your lack of organization, know that it can wreck your image and career goals.

SAVVY SUGGESTION: Look for a certified professional organizer to review everything from your phone settings to the way you have your files named. Before you hire anyone, ask for references. Talk to previous customers to make sure they were happy with the service provided and the changes made.

DAY 65

HOW TO WORK WITH THE INTERN

The recent economic climate has changed our perception of interns. Yesteryear's intern had little to no office experience and was very young. They were there to learn and do the grunt work. That is not the case today. Interns come in all shapes, sizes, age brackets and with varied experience levels. My words of caution: never underestimate the office intern.

Why?

<u>You can be replaced</u> by that cheaper worker-bee known as "the intern". You may wish you could dump any undesirable task (think typing up meeting agendas) on this person you view as the peon, but if you do, you are giving her another chance to show her worth over yours.

So, what to do?

<u>Offer advice nicely.</u> If you see her struggling with her badge to open the back door, show her that she was swiping it backwards without coming across as Mr. Cool. Offer help with a friendly smile and your full attention. It's very likely the intern will have some downtime and return the favor by offering her help to you. That's how you do things in Niceville.

Seek advice nicely. If you are over the age of, say, 50; and the intern is, well, *not*, you could probably learn a thing or two from the whippersnapper. When your cellphone magically starts vibrating when it should be ringing, ask her if she would mind lending you a hand. When your boss tells you to update your LinkedIn profile, ask for some input from her rather than wasting time trying to do it yourself.

Include her as part of the team. When it's time for a department meeting, drop by her desk to see if she knows where to go. If you are seeking input from the team on a potential change in the project timeline, ask her, too. It's not nice to exclude people. It wasn't on the playground and it's not in the office.

SAVVY SUGGESTION: Engage your office intern in conversation about work or about nothing at least once a week. You will be viewed as a leader for taking the initiative to help foster her experience.

DAY 66

How To Offer Condolences

During my very first tenure as a manager, a lady in my group experienced the terrible and unexpected death of her mother. My conscious would not let me ask her when she thought she would be back in the office, but my project calendar desperately needed to know. It can be hard to find the balance between practicality and pain. Should you find yourself in the company of bad news, bear this in mind when a task load is bearing down:

<u>Until company policy says so, the bereaved does not have to worry about work.</u> Most companies offer bereavement leave so you must respect that. It is completely unacceptable to contact an associate during their leave for work reasons.

<u>Remember cultural differences.</u> Don't assume the family would like a big arrangement of flowers and a casserole. You can ask the funeral home or a close friend for advice. Often, donations to certain charities or organizations are preferred over items offered to the family. Be aware, too, that different cultures dictate certain traditions surrounding death and bereavement. Be respectful of practices different than your own.

When the bereaved comes back to work, acknowledge their loss. You can accomplish this by a verbal expression or a hand-written note.

Be thoughtful. But, I already signed the card sent to her by our group, you may think. What would you like your coworkers to do if someone close to you died? You could gather her mail and stack it neatly on her desk or put it in a box on the floor of her office. You could go through your manager to offer help in covering unattended tasks or checking in with her clients. If you know of deadlines coming up, see what you can do to help meet that deadline.

Be patient. Your coworker is going to need some elbow room when she gets back. Likely, she will have stacks of phone messages, a ton of emails and lots on her mind. Don't run to her on the first day back asking if she has finished reviewing the report you left on her desk while she was gone.

The things you do for a coworker who is out of the office grieving is not something to brag about. Frankly, it's just what you are expected to do as a compassionate human being – not because you are Super Man.

SAVVY SUGGESTION: Offer condolences to a friend without appearing uncomfortable. Look them in the eye and don't stumble over your words. You may need to practice before getting face to face.

DAY 67

YOUR PARENTS

If you are over 35 years old, you are probably wondering why there would be a day in this book devoted to parents. If you are under 35 years old, I am quite possibly about to make you mad.

Your parents have absolutely no role in your professional life. Period.

I am constantly amazed at how often clients tell me they get calls from employee's parents. It could be they want to make sure their son, who applied for a job, supplied all the necessary paperwork. It could be they are calling in sick for their daughter. Or, it could be they are calling because they don't believe their child was treated fairly during the last performance evaluation. Do you know what amazes me even more? These employees still show up for work without a bag over their head even *after their Mommy called their boss!* Personally, I would die.

Your job is your responsibility. Your boss did not hire you with the understanding that they would be dealing with you *and* your Mom. No boss has time for all that drama. And, really, that's all it is...drama. If you are so ill that you can't call in sick for yourself, you better be on an operating table. There are enough challenges in the business world to keep your boss busy. Trust me when I tell you he is turned off big time to get a call from your Mama. What a lapse in judgment you are displaying by having anyone else perform any of your job duties.

Here is what your boss is thinking when they get a call from someone listed as your emergency contact: *How can I be sure Mrs. Helicopter Mom will not call one of my clients when Little Johnny hits a snag?* That's a big breach of trust you have to overcome. There is no way you will be considered for a task of any significance with that cloud over your head.

Your job success is firmly situated on your shoulders, so bear it strongly. Speak for yourself in clear and certain language. Pave your own road to the top without having to give your mother any credit.

SAVVY SUGGESTION: Just don't.

DAY 68

CLOSING TIME

Who doesn't sigh a little sigh of relief when the closing bell rings? It's completely natural, no matter how much you love your job, to feel a sense of relief when the workday is over. What is not ok, however, is to be the first out the door at 4:59 and a half. I can promise you that nothing bad happens from 5:00 to 5:15, so fulfill your obligation to your job and your boss by working a full workday. Working 7 hours and 55 minutes is not a full workday.

Review these 5 o'clock pitfalls to make sure you aren't letting the door hit your reputation in the ___.

- *Beginning the end of your day at 4:30.* I have worked with people who, literally, would not talk to you after 4:30. They were busy finishing up and packing up and would not be disturbed from their mission of getting out the door promptly at 5:00. These were the same ones who would walk out of a meeting at their designated lunch hour, too. I think it's safe to say their career is not too important to them.

- *Telling someone you can't do something because it is close to closing time.* When you accepted the job, you agreed to work a certain number of hours. So, do what you said you would do.

- *Using the last hour on the job to goof around.* Spending an excessive amount of time chatting with your best work buds, surfing the net, texting your pals to arrange the afternoon's cocktail hour or "cleaning your desk" are ways you waste the company's money and give the impression that your career is something you work on when it's convenient.

These pitfalls work to build a certain reputation that is hard to overcome. Imagine the laziest person you know. What would that person have to do to make you believe they are no longer lazy, but have become a go-getter or a take-charge kind of person? It would be an uphill road. Don't let yourself get complacent in a job you have had for years or get lazy in a job you simply don't enjoy. Those that can promote you beyond your current blah-blah tasks are watching for signs that you take your job seriously and will work hard for the company at every turn. You have a reputation to protect!

SAVVY SUGGESTION: Save the tasks you enjoy the most for the last hour on the job. This will keep you motivated right up to the last moment of the day.

DAY 69

HOW TO WORK WITH RUDE PEOPLE

I realize this may come as a shock to you, however…if you work with people who are consistently rude and obnoxious, you are sitting on a gold mine of opportunity. Think about it. If you are surrounded by people who are top notch performers, it's harder to shine brightly enough to catch anyone's attention. So, don't begrudge your position because you have to work with a bunch of buzzards. Be grateful you have been given an uneven playing field. You have a leg-up and may not even realize it.

I was training a group of accountants on business etiquette when this thought first came to me. It was during the first hour of the training when I talked in depth about the fact that business etiquette skills work right alongside other functions of the business to bring in new customers and increase revenue. As I moved on to the concept that each person must bear the responsibility of good behavior, I noticed that one participant had a very confused expression. During the break, he approached me with the same bewildered look on his face. "What do you do if you are the only person in the room that agrees with what you are teaching?" he asked. I told him he is pretty lucky because he was primed to get way more from the remainder of my presentation. He seemed to understand that his existing appreciation for all things civil meant he was going in to the training well ahead of his cohorts and that his Poor Me mindset was holding him back. I later learned that my new friend moved up through his organization quickly and made partner at a very young age.

If you are not the owner of the company or in the Human Resources Department, it's not your job to try to change the attitude and behavior of the people you work with. But, that doesn't mean their poor people skills can't work to your advantage. So, rather than getting all bummed out because you have been assigned a new client alongside Casey, the office bully, think about how you will gracefully accept the accolades that will surely come your way after Casey makes the new customer mad and they turn to you to help them out of a jam. It's all in how you think about it.

SAVVY SUGGESTION: Deliberately consider your behavior versus your officemate's. Who has the leg up? If it's not you, correct the problem and do it quickly.

DAY 70

WORKING IN A GREEN OFFICE

The business world has jumped into the concept of sustainability with both feet. You are likely to find stickers over light switches reminding you to turn off the lights when you leave a room, recycling bins scattered about and an office initiative to use online materials rather than print-to-read. And, thank goodness! The influence on social behaviors large companies have can be staggering. So, what if you work for one of these green companies, yet don't fully embrace eco-friendly strategies? Answer: Give and take.

- No joking. You will find yourself on the out's with most people in your group if you mock any person's effort to go green.

- Be informed before you speak. Before you make some crack about how Tim was holding up the meeting because he was slow to capture the minutes on his IPAD, you may like to know that Tim was tagged by the company president to lead a movement toward greener operating principles. What has the company president tagged you to do lately?

What if you are the office Green Machine yet your coworkers don't seem to care about the future of the earth? Answer: Give and take.

- <u>No preaching.</u> If you try to cram your message down everyone's throat, you will find greater resistance. Politely and patiently offer suggestions, but only if your subject seems receptive. The monthly group meeting is not the time to jump on your soap box.

- <u>Be informed before you speak.</u> You might like to know the gas-guzzler you would love to side-swipe in the parking lot belongs to Heather in Marketing. Since you have never met her, you wouldn't know that the inside of her gas-guzzler is modified for her since she is paralyzed from the waist down. That size car works best since she transports her wheelchair.

People do things for different reasons and you don't always get to know what those reasons are. Making a fuss about something that is not related to the function of the business or what generates your paycheck is counterintuitive. Keep your eye on the ball and be an example for others – not the thorn in their side.

<u>SAVVY SUGGESTION</u>: Come up with productive ways to promote green office practices that will showcase your initiative and creativity. Newsletters, lunch and learns, after 5 green gatherings, etc. are examples of ways you can work the cause *and* continue your real work.

DAY 71

THE COMPANY LOGO

If you have worked for any company for just about any length of time, you have all sorts of stuff with the company logo on it. Everything from beach towels to clocks proudly sport the logo you barely notice anymore.

Enter potentially damaging mind-set #1: You don't see the logo anymore. You drive past it in the parking lot, you walk past it on the door coming in to the building, your fingers cover it up when you show your badge to the security guard, you look beyond it on the motivational posters hung along the wall on the way to your office or cube and your day goes on. The same goes for the logo on the coozie you used last weekend at the concert in the park. Remember? That was the day you had just a little too much to drink and danced shirtless to the cover band's version of "Free Falling". You may not have noticed the logo that day, but I can assure you other people did.

Enter potentially damaging mind-set #2: You forget you are displaying the logo. That blue chair you take to every single one of your son's baseball games is your lucky chair, right? It's the one that got you through the play-offs last season. Well, it was the chair and the fact that you screamed at the umpire throughout the entire game. What would your son's team do without you and your lucky blue chair displaying your company's logo on the back?

In case you aren't adept at reading sarcasm, I'll be more clear. No one appreciates your antics when you are wearing or using company identifiable items. When you can be identified as a representative of any organization, you become the face of the group. Further, you become an indication of the quality of service provided by that company and the quality of the people who work there. Be mindful that you always represent the brand well.

SAVVY SUGGESTION: Just because you are given company items, does not mean you have to use them. If you do not want the burden of representing your company while performing any mundane weekend activity, go through all your closets and drawers and get rid of anything with the logo on it.

DAY 72

BE RESOURCEFUL

I hear all sorts of reasons why people do not use business etiquette skills when working as part of a group, representing a company or marketing themselves. The number one excuse I hear is *I didn't know.* That's really too bad that people will succumb to such a cop-out excuse when we are talking about something so important. If you are invited to dinner at the boss's house and don't know how to get to his neighborhood, are you going to be a no-show or are you going to get on MapQuest?

No one ever said you have to know everything. You do, however, have to be willing to find a good answer. Think outside the box when you are looking for concrete answers or simply a direction in which to move. If someone comments to you that you are always late, perhaps you should look for an alternate way to keep up with appointments. Do you always feel under-dressed? Most department stores offer complimentary personal shoppers that can make style suggestions. If you are traveling to El Paso with your boss, check with your friends on Facebook for a restaurant suggestion. All three of these scenarios and their solutions work toward making you appear in control, knowledgeable and intelligent. That describes somebody I'd like to do business with.

While a lot of people are reluctant to ask for help, it is actually a tremendous show of confidence. Eleanor Roosevelt said, "No one can make you feel inferior without your consent." Fearlessly ask those around you for their insights or suggestions, then use your own intelligence to arrive at an answer or solution.

Being resourceful implies that you are:

1. Willing to try new things

2. Open to suggestions from other people

3. Not opposed to change

4. Openminded

In our ever-changing world, these are valuable traits every person should strive to possess.

SAVVY SUGGESTION: Create a list of resources you can use when you are searching for an answer or solution. This list can be websites, blogs, apps or people.

DAY 73

HOW TO USE BUSINESS ETIQUETTE TO BOOST PRODUCTIVITY

Professionals use business etiquette as a means to an end. It's the way to get from here to there. It's a guide. Without this guide, anxiety and unease begin to limit your productivity. That is uncomfortable and no fun at all.

Take a look at these 4 ways mastering the skills of business etiquette can boost your output.

1) <u>Being comfortable gives you freedom to take advantage of unusual opportunities</u>. Someone who is comfortable in lots of different situations will not shy away from an out-of-the-box setting. Let's say your boss asks you to entertain clients for dinner who are in town from Sweden. Oh, and by the way, they don't speak English. Some might say No Way! But, the savvy and confident team player will figure it out. Get a translator, get a book on Continental Dining skills, read up on the current events in Sweden…do whatever needs to be done to get the job done. In the end, you will have impressed not only the clients, but your boss, for working to make *them* feel welcome.

2) <u>You are able to connect with anybody.</u> Let's face it, half the battle in the workplace is fitting in with the culture of the company and the people who work there. Without a pleasant working relationship with the people you spend so many hours with, you will never be viewed as a team player. In order to develop that relationship, you have to be nice and engaging. You must be able to initiate small talk, mingle with other departments during the company picnic and even offer condolences to a coworker who has experienced a tragedy.

3) <u>Presenting yourself with authority is a key ingredient for any leader.</u> If the people that work for you do not take you seriously or follow-through with their commitments, it could be because they do not view you as an authority figure. Are you sending them that message by your body language, your posture or your lack of eye contact? These are things that, if done correctly, can let everyone in the room know you are in charge without saying a word.

4) <u>Organization is a form of business etiquette.</u> It falls into the 'impression management' category. Unfortunately, the signs of un-organization can't be hidden very easily. Papers trailing behind when you walk into a room, the clutter and disarray on your desk, the scramble to find a document or file all screams lack of competence. Others will react to that impression you give off and not seek you out for projects and opportunities. It's hard to be productive when you are shunned from the action.

<u>SAVVY SUGGESTION</u>: Create your own rules of behavior that will boost your productivity. Remember to implement them!

DAY 74

PUNCTUALITY

Being late is a habit that should be broken. It's a matter of self-discipline. Your reputation as a serious professional can be lost in as little at 3 minutes. Often, people who are late are simply unorganized. It may have been a looming deadline that forced you to finish a task before breaking into a sprint on the way to a meeting. Or, it could be you simply didn't have an engagement in your calendar so you remembered at the last minute. Neither excuse is acceptable. Management will believe there is no way you can manage your workload if you can't manage your own schedule of appointments.

Being late also implies that you believe you are the most important person in the joint. Now, it's likely you don't honestly think that, but by showing such little respect for others on the guest list, that's the only conclusion to draw. If everyone else can make the choices necessary to ensure they arrive at a meeting 5 minutes early, you can do the same. Here are some tips:

- Use a calendar. No one cares if it's paper or electronic, just get one. If you are particularly forgetful, choose an electronic version so you can set reminders that will *ding!* when you need to be somewhere.

- Before you leave the office in the afternoon, review your appointments for the next day. You may even like to make a list of them so you can take it home. Tape it to your refrigerator, on your bathroom mirror or anywhere you can't miss.

- Set your alarm 20 minutes earlier than you have it today. If you start the day a few minutes behind, it will only get worse and the day goes on.

- If you have an assistant, have a conversation with her about ways she can help you get to appointments on time. Make this one area in which you are accountable to him or her.

SAVVY SUGGESTION: Hire a professional organizer to help get your workload and responsibilities organized and get all your appointments in a scheduling device. As a party unrelated to your career, this person will be able to offer comments that may seem contrary to your company culture but are still productive.

DAY 75

HOW TO WORK AMONG COMMON COURTESY

Unfortunately, common courtesies tend to take us by surprise. Is that because we have come to expect much *less* than common courtesy? Regrettably, I too am surprised when a stranger picks up something I have dropped on the sidewalk. I was traveling once when a man offered to help me lift my carry-on up into the storage bin on the airplane. I was surprised. Businesses offer courtesies under the guise of offering exceptional customer service. Individuals, however, are challenged to make it a part of their everyday living.

If you are not accustomed to dining in a nice restaurant, it can be a shock when the server reaches to place your napkin in your lap. My sister recently had dinner at The Cloister on Sea Island, an exclusive island off the coast of Georgia. When she placed her handbag on the floor beside her chair, someone quickly reached to pick it up and place it on a small wooden stool. When she told me about that, I wondered how many people may have reacted strongly thinking someone was snatching their purse!

Have you ever considered what your reactions to courtesies say about you? If you are caught off guard, you can appear defensive and suspicious. You can also lead people to assume you do not consider common courtesies relevant. If you ignore the act, you appear indifferent. Reacting in any way short of gracefully is like blowing your cover. It's like saying to the world, "I know you thought I valued kindness, but I'm really not comfortable with all that."

SAVVY SUGGESTION: Use the words "thank you" and "you're welcome" often and deliberately. Don't water it down by using "thanks" and "no problem" instead.

DAY 76

MINE OR NOT?

Some items you become accustomed to using in the office can grow to feel like your own. *Your* pen, the one you use every day because you like the clip on the side and the point size. *Your* chair, the one that was at *your* desk when you started that job 8 years ago. *Your* lunch hour, the 11:00 hour you have always taken because of your seniority. You begin to view co-workers as family (think love/hate relationship) and equipment as worthy of your monogram (think masking tape bearing your initials and stuck to your stapler).

It's easy to forget who actually owns these items. Who paid for the binder you claim as your own? Who got the invoice for all those multi-colored paper clips that keep you so organized?

Not recognizing the ways you can unintentionally steal from your company can lead you down a very unethical road. Take note of the ways you can lead management to wonder about your level of honesty:

- **Office supplies**: While it's ok to make a request for a certain item that you believe will enable you to be more efficient, it is not ok to make a request based on personal preference. If you prefer gel tip pens over ball point, go buy the gels yourself. Also, "forgetting" to remove supplies from your briefcase and letting your kids use them for school projects is dishonest.

- **Time**: Overstating your time sheet is wrong. If you came back from lunch 5 minutes late, write that in.

- **Perks**: Educate yourself on the boundaries of company perks. If baseball tickets are available at a discount for employees, don't buy them for your girlfriend's parents.

- **Time off**: It is unethical to call in sick if you are not sick or say you have a doctor's appointment when you are actually heading out to the beach for the afternoon.

- **Information**: You are privy to certain company information because you are employed by that company and they believe you will follow the policy regarding company privacy. To spout off proprietary information at a party or on the golf course will only make you look immature and obnoxious. Neither of these traits are admirable.

SAVVY SUGGESTION: Look through your desk and briefcase. Are there items you need to return to the supply closet? When talking about company business, remember this: less is more.

DAY 77

CROSS-TRAINING

As businesses deal with the challenges of a struggling economy, they look for ways to become more efficient. Cross-training employees is a no brainer. Rather than paying 4 employees to perform similar yet separate job tasks, it makes financial sense to cross-train 3 of the employees and eliminate the expense of the fourth. Did you catch the *big-picture* approach to this *business* decision to cross-train employees?

The pitfall so often seen by employers with regard to cross-training is the group's attitude. Don't be a killjoy. Embrace the opportunity to learn a new aspect of the company's operation. Take a look at these no-no's when it comes to working as part of a team:

- You don't really care to know how to perform any other function? It is your prerogative to have that opinion, but it's the company's prerogative to prevent you from expressing it. Everybody is working toward to same goal – company success ie receiving a paycheck – so do your part and do not complain.

- Do not use cross-training as an excuse when a customer makes a request of you. It is terribly inappropriate to say to a customer *I don't usually work in this area, so I don't know.* Simply say, *Let me get that answer for you.*

- Never gripe around the water cooler about your boss asking you to do things you "weren't hired to do." When you were hired, it's likely the company saw something in you that implied you were up for any challenge and ready to work. Leading a gripe session will ruin your reputation in no time flat.

- Tackle learning your new tasks with gusto. This secondary position should be viewed to be as relevant to your career as the position you were hired to fulfill. What you will learn is resume-worthy, so don't let yourself down by not learning and performing at top speed.

SAVVY SUGGESTION: If you have not been asked to cross-train within your organization, ask for the opportunity. Your boss will love you for inquiring!

DAY 78

SOMEONE ELSE WILL DO IT

Isn't it frustrating to find the postage machine with only a dollar left on it or the recycle bins overflowing because the papers are stacked haphazardly making them spill over the edges? These may seem like menial tasks that you are way over-qualified to worry about, but no one is remembering where you got your MBA if you are the one to let the phone ring off the hook while you eat your sandwich.

The thought *someone else will do it* should stop you dead in your tracks. Recognizing something should be done and doing it is an office courtesy. It truly is a shame to let opportunity slide by when you choose to let someone else do something you could just as easily do yourself.

Case in point: During my freshman year of college, I rear-ended a lady on my way to buy something I needed for that night's formal. I'll leave out any mention of my running late or the Talking Heads playing a touch too loudly. Standing on Briarcliff Road on a sunny Saturday afternoon in Atlanta as my hair and clothes blew in the wind of the traffic, I was tempted to call my Dad and let him do all the talking. However, I pushed through and dealt with the situation myself. As it turned out, I rear-ended a very nice producer at

CNN who invited me to tour the station, to lunch and to meet some CNN "stars". Wow. Had I cowered, stood back and handed my bag phone (yes, a bag phone) to this lady to speak to my dad, I would have missed out on a wonderful experience and lovely friendship.

The single greatest thing you can do to promote yourself and your career is to show initiative. As you repeatedly decide to take on new projects, seek out new relationships and prove your worth inside an organization or project team, your value will grow exponentially. The added benefit is that your own feeling of self worth will feed your confidence and your adventuresome side. Don't be lazy. Be courteous.

SAVVY SUGGESTION: Identify one office or customer service task you hate doing. Now, come up with a creative and new way of completing the task. Complete the task the new way 3 times. Are you on to something you should share with your officemates or even your boss?

DAY 79

CHANGE IS A GOOD THING

"That's not what I was hired to do."

"That's not what they told me."

"Why would they tell us to do that?"

These are common responses when management introduces change. Anything from a change in dress code to a change in how often the janitorial staff appears can create chatter that leads to dissent. Before you find a soap box, consider exactly how this change will impact your life. If you can't find an impact to yourself, keep your mouth shut. There are people who love change and there are people who panic when they see change coming. Nothing productive comes from a panic attack, so listen up.

Change is a good thing. Where there is change, there is opportunity. If your company has been bought out by an international conglomerate and you don't speak Italian or Japanese, is it really just to fault the company for seizing a growth opportunity? You should be glad to be with a company who is moving forward. And, who doesn't want to go to Italy?? It's unlikely you would have taken up a second language in your free time, so seize the opportunity and be grateful for the boost to your resume.

The worst thing you could do for yourself when change is imminent is to appear as if you don't want to go along. That means when meetings are held to discuss what you can expect or to make announcements, watch your facial expression. Don't scowl. Also, watch that you don't become guilty of nay-saying because of the people you hang around. Distance yourself from the outspoken ones who speak out of turn and badmouth management.

SAVVY SUGGESTION: When change is coming your way, be the model nomad. Take your ingenuity and your sensibility anywhere the company needs you and knock their socks off.

DAY 80

BUILDING BUSINESS RELATIONSHIPS

If you enter any career with the understanding that relationships are the foundation of business, you will lead a happy and healthy existence. Building those relationships is a huge component in your job success. After all, you spend the majority of the hours of your day with the people you work with. It stands to reason that you need to fit in and be accepted as part of the team.

- <u>Speak to everybody, everywhere, all the time.</u> This isn't brown-nosing the boss or sucking up to the media room clerk so you get your copies quicker. This is being personable and engaging. It's rude to walk down the hall or through the lobby without acknowledging other people. All it takes is a smile and a wave and you will have "spoken".

- <u>Speak to everyone in the same manner.</u> Don't save your heartiest and warmest affections for the boss. That *is* sucking up. Others will question your validity on a whole host of issues if they see you put on such a false bravado. At the same time, offer a genuine greeting to the meekest of associates. Reaching to the bottom of the totem pole is viewed as a confident and mature move.

- <u>Accept diversity with ease.</u> People are different. Don't make jokes or use nicknames related to ethnic differences. It is passe, short-sighted and a sign of ignorance. Do you think you will be asked to travel internationally if you do such a good job of offending those on your own doorstep?

- <u>Know when it's time to apologize.</u> Accidents happen either by the tongue or the hand. And, when an accident happens, an apology is usually in order. Let's say you spill your coffee on your cube-mate's briefcase. Certainly, clean up the mess, but don't let that stand as the apology. Consider writing a note expressing your regret. This makes the mishap much easier to tolerate. If you inadvertently offend someone with a snide remark or off-color joke, a verbal apology is required immediately. Don't wait a few days. Express your remorse within the hour.

- <u>Give credit where it is due.</u> Stealing someone's thunder and/or ideas is unethical. If you are serious about your career path and the longevity of your brand, you will not do this.

SAVVY SUGGESTION Consider the line of business you are in and the people you work with. Now, think of strategies to connect with them in ways that will promote them and your company. Expressing appreciation with a hand-written note or a phone call is quick, effective and always well-received. And, it's just *nice*.

FROM HERE

You did it! Congratulations! You devoted 1 minute per day for 16 weeks to bettering your life and your career. My last instruction to you now is to *go forth*! Don't just *be*. Be the rock star you know you are. Shine. Influence. Spread it. Pay it forward. Be bold. Now you know how to maneuver where most people get bogged down, so what are you waiting for? Strike out into a new day with a new mission.

Your mind-set has gone from 'What's in it for me?' to 'How can I help?' and this will make your career skyrocket. TOMS Shoes is a great example of how this mind-set can be the basis for a company's success. Their tagline is 'With every pair you purchase, TOMS will give a pair of new shoes to a child in need.' They call it 'One for One'. After hearing that, who doesn't want to do business with this company? They celebrated the company's 4th birthday in May of 2010 with One for One Act of Kindness Day. This movement was designed to inspire people to perform an act of kindness for someone. Consumers are drawn to this balance between the bottom line and social consciousness. It makes the company seem like a person. A person who has values and concerns. A person you would like to get to know. TOMS is popular with nearly all age groups because while they provide a quality product, they also engage their customers on a very personal level. As I've said before, people do business with people they like and people *like* TOMS Shoes.

Rewards will come your way when your heart and mind are in the right place. Be a good steward of your talents, goals, dreams and aspirations. Put yourself out there in a way that allows and even encourages others to follow you. Putting your business etiquette skills to work is not being showy.

Remember, this is not about coercing or scheming. This is about being organically nice so your mere presence is irresistible. In doing so, the business will follow and your bottom line will grow.

THE SECRET INGREDIENTS

Business etiquette is not a simple list of do's and don'ts. Business etiquette requires a certain mind-set. Being able to put into play the rules provided in this book requires discretion, compassion and patience.

1. It requires discretion because no two situations are alike and society keeps throwing us curveballs. You have to be ready to dig out one or more rules of etiquette that will guide you through and when all else fails, fall back to The Golden Rule. As long as your effort is genuine, you will leave the superb impression you set out to give.

2. It requires compassion because true etiquette dictates you put other's needs and desires ahead of your own. Sometimes it's hard to put others before yourself – particularly when you are struggling to show your worth. It's better to not be known by the management team at all than to be known for something unfavorable.

3. It requires patience because etiquette in the workplace dictates that you not behave obnoxiously. That means you may have to wait a while for the squeaky wheels to be serviced before you are noticed. But, it will be worth the wait, because while others are behaving like a bull in a china shop, you will have been using the nuances of the etiquette world to blow the minds of your office mates and customers.

Put your own personal flair toward showing discretion, compassion and patience as you build your career. Just don't fake it - nobody likes a rat.

Using Kate's Quips

If you are serious about long-term professional success, consider these one-liners your prompt or rather your signal to act. Implementing behavioral change requires a mind-set shift and using these remarks will help you accomplish just that. How? Because using these in an effective and methodical way will drip this new method of operating into your psyche on a regular basis until it becomes your new way of thinking. Everybody could stand constant reminding when it comes to evaluating yourself and your progress. It's not always comfortable to take a good hard look at yourself. Regardless, you are a winner for getting this far, so you know that self-evaluation is a necessary evil but with it comes the ultimate professional success. To push ahead of your competition, make using your new business etiquette skills as easy as possible by using Kate's Quips in whatever ways work for you. Here are some ideas:

- Jot these Quips on post-it notes and stick several around your home and office. Visual reminders tend to make a bigger impression on us. Be sure to change them out every few days.

- Use Outlook (or some other software) to create an automated reminder containing a Quip rather than an appointment. Schedule these at different times during the week so you won't come to expect them.

- If you use a traditional paper daytimer, take a few minutes to write a Quip into several days over the course of the year.

- Write a Quip on a notecard and prop it up over the time display on your alarm clock. Put it there at night so it's the first thing you see when you wake up.

- If you prepare your lunch at home, slip yourself a Quip to be read each day while you eat. This is a wonderful mid-day boost!

- Find an accountability partner (friend, relative, mentor, etc.). Text Quips to each other at unexpected times.

- Choose a Quip and write about it in your blog. This will force you to (again) carefully consider the intent of good behavior.

- Insert Quips in your project or customer relationship management tool. Choose ones that will be relevant at specific points in the life of the client or project.

KATE'S QUIPS

Having nice manners is not about perfection. It's about knowing the rules of etiquette well enough to display grace under pressure.

Nothing says *I've got it going on* like knowing how to present yourself to another person.

Having poor people skills in business is a distraction that no one can afford when it's time to make a deal.

People take you at your actions and your words. Both speak loudly and clearly.

In business, it matters how we view and act on the needs of others, it matters how we behave, and it matters that we are nice.

If showing no couth and grace at work is the silent killer, then doing your job with compassion, patience and discretion is your highway to heaven.

In business, it's the weak ties that bind, so make sure they are singing your praises.

Possessing the skills necessary to be marketable and, at the very least, pleasant to be around is practical and necessary in business.

Superb communication and interpersonal skills are among the most important characteristics a professional should possess.

Business etiquette pulls everything together by ensuring one displays respect, civility and consideration.

Preparation is one big-time element of success...and helps you show off your business etiquette. Being prepared allows you to relax so you can present yourself as confident and competent. Swirling around like a stressed out tornado makes everyone uneasy.

Would you hire you?

The goal of a good introduction is to make yourself look good and the other people feel good.

A lot of people have a mid-week slump on Wednesdays. Do something unexpected for someone who needs a lift. Make somebody smile!

Inhaling to get all the good stuff off the spoon is the same thing as slurping. It just is.

The art of making conversation is very nearly a lost art. Find a few sources of interesting information that is not weighed down in misery so you can be well-read and informed. Your clients and your friends will see the difference!

Without abiding by the rules of business etiquette, you are shooting in the dark when it comes to connecting with people.

Connecting with people is one key to career success, so don't alienate yourself because you think you are always right.

Manic Monday advice: stay calm, get organized and mind your manners. You got this.

Don't mince words at the office. Be concise, be clear, be strong and be confident.

Products and services are what lead you to a company, but it's the people that will keep you there.

Look at yourself in the mirror head to toe. How's that impression management thing going?

When is the last time you struck up a conversation with at stranger? Practice, practice.

Go to www.alltop.com and make a list of conversation starters. This blog directory updates daily so there is something for everyone.

You are a cut above trivial office hype and complaints. It's likely the topic is not relevant to your job performance and there is no way your participation can make you look good.

Be open-minded when hearing criticism and learn from another's perspective. To stop learning is to put a cap on your earnings potential.

The truth about character building: You have to work at it.

Business etiquette may seem trivial when you are talking about a multi-million dollar deal, but it's the influence these details have on the relationship with your customer that matter.

Prior to your next meeting, think of one thing you can do to show you are being considerate of everyone's time and effort.

There is power in simply being. The trick is in the *how*.

The power of your presence is in your maturity, integrity and judgment.

It can be a chore to ensure your behavior mimics your character, but the rewards are well worth the effort.

If you are unemployed, keep a journal of daily activities so you can make sure you are staying productive.

Don't preach. Be the example.

When you have an earpiece attached to you, it's like carrying a big sign that says *I am unavailable.*

Is your multi-tasking helping or hurting your image?

There is no room in business for anything less than an energetic and inspired disposition.